Forschungen zum Alten Testament

herausgegeben von
Bernd Janowski und Hermann Spieckermann

2

Text and Concept in Leviticus 1:1−9

A Case in Exegetical Method

von

Rolf P. Knierim

J. C. B. Mohr (Paul Siebeck) Tübingen

ROLF P. KNIERIM was born 1928; he studied Theology 1950−55; 1948−50 and 1955−59 he was in Church Ministry; 1957 Promotion, 1958−63 Assistant and Lecturer Old Testament in Heidelberg, 1963 Habilitation, 1963−66 Lecturer in Heidelberg; since 1966 Professor of Old Testament, School of Theology at Claremont, and Avery Professor of Religion, Claremont Graduate School.

Die Deutsche Bibliothek – CIP-Einheitsaufnahme

Knierim, Rolf P.:
Text and concept in Leviticus 1:1−9: a case in exegetical method / von Rolf P. Knierim. – Tübingen: Mohr, 1992
   (Forschungen zum Alten Testament; 2)
   ISBN 3-16-145859-1
NE: GT

© 1992 by J. C. B. Mohr (Paul Siebeck), P. O. Box 2040, D-7400 Tübingen.

The book was typeset by Gulde-Druck in Tübingen using Times typeface, printed by Gulde-Druck in Tübingen on acid free stock paper from Papierfabrik Buhl in Ettlingen and bound by Heinr. Koch in Tübingen.

Printed in Germany.

ISSN 0940-4155

Foreword

This study focuses on a particular aspect of exegetical method. Rather than abstractly discussing the theory of method, it concretely applies this aspect to the actual exegesis of a text. In the process, exegetical method and actual exegesis – are intended to – complement and control each other. This format also lends itself to a more direct dialogue with those publications on the same text in which methodology and exegesis interpenetrate in relevant ways.

At issue is the relationship in a text between its statement and its thought, between what is explicit and what is implicit, between what a text expresses and what is operative in, and even the presupposition for, that text, although it is not expressed. Texts not only speak, they also think as they speak. They are not simply story, but thoughtful story. Indeed, and this must certainly be said for the written biblical texts, they are in many respects the result of intensive intellectual processes into which considerable critical discernment was invested before, and for, making the decision regarding what had to be put into writing, and how it was to be put into writing. In this study, the relationship between a text's expression and its implicit thought is called Text and Concept.

The encounter with this issue in exegetical publications, or in the entire arena of biblical interpretation for that matter, is not new. It has never been avoidable. In more recent developments, it has surfaced in one way or another in virtually every established exegetical method. Yet the way in which the relationship between the text and its concept is handled is all too often more coincidental than methodologically conscious. This demonstrates not so much the violation of method by exegetes as a certain deficit of the method itself, within which this aspect is not sufficiently located in its own right.

That the exegetical process starts at the individuality of the extant text is based on the fact that each text exists first of all in its individual kind. However, this starting point is by no means intended to replace the study of the text's typical features, especially its genre and setting and their tradition history. It only means that a more controlled discernment of the text's genre may be attained after, rather than before, all factors of its individual nature are taken into account. Consequently, the starting point in the present study at the text's individuality is just as advisable as the subsequent discussion of its genre is necessary.

The choice of Lev 1:1−9 is coincidental. This text is merely a case for the same focus which is necessary for all texts. Whatever the hoped for merits of the results of our study may be for our understandig of this specific text, the results themselves point to what may be exegetically achieved for all texts. Should the relationship between text and concept play more than a coincidental or peripheral role, this focus may affect the system of our exegetical method more than has been realized thus far.

I wish to express my admiration for and indebtedness to the editors of the *Forschungen zum Alten Testament,* professors Bernd Janowski and Hermann Spieckermann, and the publisher, Georg Siebeck, for their daring consent to publish this study written in English so early in their new series.

In Claremont, I am indebted to Marilyn Lundberg, senior Old Testament Ph.D. student and my former research associate at the Institute for Antiquity and Christianity, for editing the manuscript, to Randy Merritt and Michael Phelps, senior Old Testament Ph.D. students and my current research associates, for their extensive contribution to additional editorial work and for creating the indices, to Cynthia Eades for word-processing, and to her husband Keith, also a senior Old Testament Ph.D. student, for voluntary assistance. Claremont Graduate School, the Institute for Antiquity and Christianity, and the School of Theology at Claremont have provided various kinds of support without which even a short scholarly book could scarcely be carved out from an otherwise full professional schedule. Last but not least, the distinction between writing and instruction discussed in this study also applies to the different settings in which the study itself has been encountered: alone at my desk, and in the classroom with the doctoral students of my seminar. For the former and its purpose, the responsibility is mine alone. Regarding the latter, quite different, setting and purpose, I cannot but always be impressed by the commitment of these men and women to intensive exegetical labor, and thankful for our learning together.

Claremont, California
September, 1991   Rolf P. Knierim

Table of Contents

Abbreviations

I. Miscellaneous abbreviations

BB	*Das Bundesbuch* (The Covenant Book)
Diss.	Dissertation
H	*Das Heiligkeitsgesetz* (The Holiness Code)
imperf.	imperfect
MT	Massoretic Text
P	Priestly Source
perf.	perfect
pers.	person
plur.	plural
sing.	singular

II. Publications

ATD	Das Alte Testament Deutsch
FRLANT	Forschungen zur Religion und Literatur des Alten und Neuen Testaments
HAT	Handbuch zum Alten Testament
HUCA	*Hebrew Union College Annual*
JPS	Jewish Publication Society
JSOTSup	Journal for the Study of the Old Testament-Supplement Series
NICOT	New International Commentary on the Old Testament
OBO	Orbis biblicus et orientalis
RSV	*Revised Standard Version*
THAT	E. Jenni and C. Westermann (eds.), *Theologisches Handwörterbuch zum Alten Testament*
TWAT	G. J. Botterweck and H. Ringgren (eds.), *Theologisches Wörterbuch zum Alten Testament*
WMANT	Wissenschaftliche Monographien zum Alten und Neuen Testament

Introduction

It has always been observed in biblical exegesis that the texts contain not only statements but also presuppositions. The surface level of a text communicates to the reader explicit information, but it also points to aspects beneath itself which are, nevertheless, implicitly operative in it and which generate and control its form and content. Texts are linguistic semantic entities in which explicit statements and their presuppositions interact. Exegesis must, therefore, do more than paraphrase what a text says. It must also, however hypothetically, reconstruct a text's assumptions which lie underneath its surface.[1] It must explain its system, its *Gestalt,* if for no other reason than to help us achieve a better understanding of the text's statements. In doing so, it must distinguish between the critical paraphrase of the text's message and the reconstruction of its assumptions, and attempt to explain the relationship of both and their mutual convertibility.

The message of a text and its assumptions are mutually convertible. This is especially true for the relationship between a text and those of its assumptions that are conceptual in nature. However, in order that we

---

[1] Some terminological distinctions are necessary for this study. The term "reconstruction" is, together with "deconstruction," frequently used in the arena of biblical hermeneutics for the reordering of dismantled = deconstructed biblical thought-systems, e.g., the system of patriarchy. This type of deconstruction and reconstruction is done in the process of reinterpreting the Bible for our modern time. In a similar sense, but also for the change of forms and contents within the biblical transmission history, terms such as "transformation" and "recontextualization" are used. In this publication, I prefer to employ the following terminological distinctions: "transformation" refers most generally to either the contextual or conceptual change of both form and/or content, in the process of innerbiblical transmission. "Recontextualization" refers to the adaptation of a given or traditional text and its concept into a new socio-historical context which is considered analogous to the old so that no conceptual change happens. "Reconceptualization" refers to the reordering of a biblical thought-system itself in the innerbiblical transmission history, but especially in its adaptation by modern interpreters for our time. As in the case of recontextualization, reconceptualization is complemented by deconceptualization. In distinction to these terms, the term "reconstruction," without the complementary notion of "deconstruction," is used specifically for the exegetical attempt to discover the presupposed but inexplicit assumptions or the conceptuality underneath a text.

may determine the relationship of these two factors, each must be recognized in its distinctiveness. The reconstruction of biblical "ideas" or "concepts" or "patterns," and the focus on them in the study of the Bible, is valid in its own right and for its own purposes, apart from its function in the exegesis of texts — as long as it does not replace, or claim to replace, that exegesis. But apart from the fact that various types of reconstruction — via texts — aim at scholarly interpretations of world-view systems for their own sake, they demand a virtually complete body of literature rather than individual texts or confined groups of texts. While the "ideas" or "concepts" or "patterns" of worldview systems play a role in the so-called deep structure of texts, they neither self-evidently, nor necessarily, represent the concepts or assumptions (or assumed concepts and conceptual assumptions) that belong to the immediate reason for and meaning of an individual text, or of a coherent group of texts, or of a larger literary work. The conceptualities that are operative in the immediacy of a text are directly important for exegetical work. They represent the focus of the present study.

A *caveat* needs to be kept in mind, namely, the danger of circular argumentation in the determination of the relationship between text and concept. This danger always exists. But the possibility or danger of circular argumentation invalidates neither the basic necessity for deter-mining the relationship between text and concept nor the legitimacy of hypothetically reconstructing a concept from a text. While reconstruc-tion necessary for understanding is inevitably hypothetical, a hypothesis is better than none at all. Our option consists of the alternative between more or less substantiated hypotheses, not between a hypothesis or no hypothesis. The danger of circular argumentation is at any rate allevi-ated by the fact that the reconstruction, to whatever extent it can facilitate a better understanding of the text, is controlled by what the text permits.[2] Texts are more than lists of independent words (lexemes) and chains of unrelated sentences (syntagms). They are held together by supra-syntagmatic factors which constitute their entity. These factors are signaled by the grammatical and syntactical *cohesion* of the surface-

---

[2] An updated study of the role which either the neglect of or attention to the presupposi-tions operative in the messages of the texts has played in the history of exegesis, beyond what is generally known and in addition to the developments generated by the fields of, e.g., form criticism, linguistics, semiotics, and structuralism, would be very instructive methodologically.

texts, while their *coherence* is conceptual in nature.[3] Whereas particular terms or statements on the surface of the text often point to these conceptualities, the concepts themselves are basically *infratextual.* And their typology is heterogeneous. A concept governing a text may be, e.g., genre-, style-, or situation-specific; it may be a particular theme, plot, concern, or intention. Its presence beneath the surface of a text may be strictly pericope-immanent, i.e., *intratextual,* but it may also be determined *contextually* as in larger literary works, or *intertextually* as in the coherence of separate literary works or documents,[4] or even *supratextually* as, e.g., by certain worldview concepts. It may be traditional or new.

Of course, many existing studies pay attention to conceptuality. Among those that directly focus on the relationship between text and concept are interpretations concerned primarily with the composition or structure of identified literary works or biblical books. This is not the place for presenting a review on the surge of interest in the composition or structure of texts, on the different approaches and findings, or on a methodology of composition-analysis. Suffice it to say that, e.g., the interpretations of the composition of the Pentateuch or of parts of it in the recent works of E. Blum, H. Utzschneider, J. Milgrom, R. P. Knierim, and others, differ considerably. It is the difference in approaches and results that is a matter of concern at this moment, rather than the question of who is more or less correct. In any case, it seems that the interpretation of the composition of texts cannot ignore the relationship between text and concept but must consciously face it.

Last but not least, discernible individual pericopes exist in their own right. In the biblical literature they are usually parts of compositions or works, and the influence of context on them must not be ignored. Nevertheless, they are units in their own right, and sometimes reveal their individuality even in tension with their context. While it is certainly legitimate to start the exegetical process of a larger literary work with the explanation of its macro-structure or -composition and subsequently to move to the explanation of its parts, it is equally legitimate to reverse that exegetical process because either process will ultimately control the

---

[3] For the helpful distinction between *Kohäsion* (cohesion) and *Kohärenz* (coherence), see H. UTZSCHNEIDER (15−16, etc.).

[4] Cf., e.g., the coherence of psalms which belong to the same group or genre, or of separate prophetic books which are based on the theological system of the deuteronomistic redactors.

results of the other. Specifically, however, an individual pericope in
principle may, and often does, have a distinct focus which sets it apart
even from such pericopes to which it belongs generically. And its distinctive individuality includes the relationship between its text and its concept or conceptual aspects. For this reason alone, exegetical work needs
to inquire into the relationship of text and concept in individual
pericopes as well as in larger works. It is, after all, not impossible that an
outside concept controlling the interpretation of a pericope may obscure
or even destroy its individuality.

The following study of Lev 1: 1–9 ventures into the direction just
mentioned. If anything justifies this quest at the outset, it is the fact that
the texts about the עלה, the burnt offering, are on several grounds clearly
distinguishable. They individually focus on different subtypes of the
same עלה. They may, and to a certain extent do, presuppose and indicate
a common עלה pattern. But they are first of all the obvious result of a
differentiated understanding of, and need for presenting, the subtypes,
the different "cases" of the עלה sacrifice, rather than the common
pattern itself. While the comparison of all subtypes and the interpretation of the entire עלה system is important, the degree and perhaps the
quality of its reconstruction may be significantly enhanced by the exegesis of the conceptual nature of the distinctly individual texts.

These introductory remarks are only meant to focus attention on the
distinction between text (specifically, surface text) and concept in the
following study. The study itself, as an exemplar, and also the literature
referred to will be concerned with highlighting this distinction more than
with presenting a complete register of all exegetical data. These data are,
at any rate, discussed in the relevant commentaries, monographs, and
articles.

§1 Lev 1:1−9 within 1:1−3:17

In the extant text, Lev 1:1−9 is part of the macro-unit 1:1−3:17. This unit is a report of a Yahweh speech to Moses. It consists of two parts: the narrator's − expanded − introductory report formula (*about* a Yahweh speech) in 1:1, and his quotation *of* the speech itself to Moses in 1:2−3:17.[5] For the interpretation of the setting and intention of the text it is as important to note that the entire unit 1:1−3:17 is simply a report about a Yahweh speech to Moses mediated by the narrators who speak *about* Moses − and not a Yahweh speech without that mediation − as it is to note that the reported instructions themselves from 1:2, especially v. 2aβ on, were given by Yahweh himself, and not by "the priests" of the priestly writings. The text does not even have a statement, let alone a report, about Moses' compliance with Yahweh's command given to him in v. 2aα.[6] Nevertheless, it certainly presupposes that compliance. And the conceptual nature of this presupposition should be assumed as implicitly operative in the text in view of the fact that the priestly literature reports such obedient compliances as one of the mainstays of its theology. That this conceptual presupposition coincides with the absence of a reference to it in the context means at least, whatever its inscrutable specific reasons may have been, that for the chain of transmission of the following laws (given for Israel's permanent existence rather than the commands given for the immediate execution of acute actions such as the building of the sanctuary, the ordination of Aaron, the judgment against Nadab and Abihu and against the blasphemer, and the organization of the camp) the emphasis on their origin was so

---

[5] For different subdivisions cf., e.g., K. ELLIGER (27); G. J. WENHAM (48−49). R. RENDTORFF's "Auf die Anrede folgt der Befehl zur Weitergabe" (1985: 23) needs reformulation. V. 1 contains no *Anrede;* it contains at best, in v. 1a, a reporting *reference to* a personal address (such as "Moses"), a reference that presupposes the address, and in v. 1b a reporting reference to the entire following speech. For the stylistic observations and their redaction historical implications here and in the following text, see the commentaries.

[6] In Leviticus, such reports or statements of compliance occur only within the contexts of Lev 8−10 and 24:10−23, in 16:34b, and in an indirect statement in 26:46.

decisive that their content quoted in the extant text was sufficient evidence for their mediation through Moses so that this mediation did not have to be explicitly mentioned.

The modern exegetical assumption that the laws about the rituals were originally created by priests means that the redactors created a hermeneutical shift by presupposing that their priestly laws about the sacrificial rituals originated in Yahweh's own instructions. According to this hermeneutical shift these instructions were given immediately after Yahweh occupied the tent of meeting, and before he gave any other instructions to Moses who (by conceptual implication) transmitted them to Aaron and his sons, our redactors. This shift, undoubtedly intended to absolutize the authority of the redactors' laws, amounts to more than a mere *recontextualization* of the same concept of the cultic laws. It amounts to a twofold *reconceptualization:* the laws themselves are Yahweh's laws and no longer priestly laws, and the authorization for the priests to transmit the laws and to perform the rituals depends on the mediation of the laws through the authority of Moses at Sinai and no longer on their own priestly tradition and authority.[7] The priests were no longer lawgivers or instructors of laws; they were reporters of received laws.

The phrase מאהל מועד in v. 1bβ deserves particular attention. It is an explicit signal for the macro-structure of the entire Sinai narrative. After the tabernacle had been erected and the cloud had covered it and the כבוד filled it (Exod 40), Yahweh no longer called Moses from Mt. Sinai but now from the tent of meeting.[8] This signal points to the concept of the movement of the Yahweh revelation from the mountain to the tent, which is clearly operative on the contextual level itself and which reflects the tradition history about the relationship between Sinai and Israel's central sanctuary.[9]

Our focus on vv. 1–9 in Lev 1 does not mean that these verses represent, or ever were, a self-contained pericope. They represent only the beginning of the Yahweh speech report which continues after 1:9

---

[7] For the interpretation of the *"Orakel-Konzept"* of these Mosaic-priestly instructions, see H. UTZSCHNEIDER (148–149).

[8] See R. P. KNIERIM (1985: 404–405).

[9] For Lev 1:1 as well as for Exod 24:16–18 it is true that Moses must wait until he is called, so K. KOCH (1959: 45); B. JANOWSKI (313); R. RENDTORFF (1985: 22). The relevant difference, however, for the composition of the Sinai narrative, is that in Exod 24:16–18 and 25:1 Moses is called from the top of the mountain whereas in Lev 1:1 he is called from the tent of meeting.

until 3:17. An interpretation of the composition itself of 1:1−3:17 would have to address all its pertinent factors, which is not our aim. But it is necessary to include attention to the introductory statements in vv. 1 and 2aα in the discussion of the first specific unit, vv. 3−9 (which is our aim) because these two introductory statements, redactional as they are, may have affected the original text of the body of the following units; and they have certainly cast a hierarchic semantic structure over that body which affects it conceptually. As will be discussed later, the question of the generic identity of the texts contained in the quoted Yahweh speech is thereby affected. E.g., as far as the notion of "instruction" is concerned, it seems at the outset that this instruction is envisioned as a one time event in which the only instructor is Yahweh. Yahweh orally instructs Moses about laws concerning sacrificial rituals. Vv. 2aβ + b and 3−9 contain the first of these. This impression, however, is only gained from vv. 1 and 2aα, and also from the 2nd pers. plur. forms in v. 2aβ + b which belong to the redactors' hands. The text from v. 3 on is not, at least not self-evidently, formulated in specifically instruction language, i.e., language that points to an instructional setting. The interpretation of the texts from v. 3 on as "instruction" seems either influenced by the instruction language of their introductory context in vv. 1, 2aα + b, which does not mean that their own language is self-evidently instruction language; or it rests on the grounds of our reconstructions of transmission historical processes behind those texts rather than on the characteristics of their own language. We need to be aware of these distinctions so that our focus on the material from v. 2aβ + b and vv. 3−9 on is not blurred by *a priori* exegetical assumptions.

§2 Lev 1:2 aα within 1:2−3:17

The second part of the macro-unit, 1:2−3:17, the quoted Yahweh speech, also consists of two parts: Yahweh's commission of Moses in v. 2 aα to promulgate what follows to the Israelites, and the content of the commanded promulgation, now given to him in 1:2 aβ−3:17. With regard to v. 2 aα we again note the implicit presupposition operative in the text, namely, that this content must have been orally transmitted by Moses to the Israelites, or it would not be known and its text could not exist. This observation is simple, but its explanation is complex and will not be pursued at this point. Suffice it to say that the text and its context imply an *infratextual* or *subtextual* conceptuality which must be rooted in the importance of the tradition-history of the Moses-concept for the priestly writers' claim to their own cultic legitimacy, even exclusivity, not only as the practitioners of the sacrifices but especially, and primarily, as the heirs and guardians of Yahweh's instructions to Moses for the Israelites.

§3 Lev 1:2aβ + b and 3–9

The content of the quoted Yahweh speech to Moses will be the actual object of this study, whereby we will confine ourselves to vv. 2aβ–9 as the paradigm for pursuing the questions raised in the introduction.

Before discussing vv. 2aβ–9 specifically, we need to identify the place of these verses within the macro-unit 1:1–3:17. Its structure appears as follows:

Report of a Yahweh speech to Moses	1:1–3:17
I. The narrator's introductory report formula	1:1
II. His quotation of the speech	1:2–3:17
A. The commissioning of Moses	1:2aα
B. The content of the commission: on קרבן	1:2aβ–3:17
1. Concerning עלה	1:2aβ–17
2. Concerning מנחה	2:1–16
3. Concerning זבח שלמים	3:1–17[10]

The subsection II.B.1. = 1:2aβ–17, concerning the עלה, is further subdivided into two parts:

1.a. The main case	vv. 2aβ + b[11]
1.b. Three subordinate cases	vv. 3–17
1) Concerning בקר	vv. 3–9
2) Concerning צאן	vv. 10–13
3) Concerning עוף	vv. 14–17

The statement about the main case, 1.a. = v. 2aβ + b, expresses an aspect that belongs to the entire section on the עלה, 1.b. = vv. 3–17, and to each of its subcases. It is not an abstraction of them, but introduces the

---

[10] The systematized order of this content, B., and also the problem of its arrangement are discussed in the pertinent publications.

[11] The signals in the text for this placing of the "main case" together with the עלה-unit are ambiguous. According to its literal statement, v. 2aβ + b could function as an introduction to the entire macro-unit, B., on קרבן. However, that unit in the extant text is interrupted by Lev 2, to which 1:2aβ + b does not refer, and the content of the apodosis in 1:2b is in part resumed in 3:1, so that 1:2aβ + b seems in the extant text to function specifically as the introduction to 1:3–17.

condition and the first regulation common to each of them. With this in mind, we can focus on vv. 2aβ−9.

Before any other consideration of structure and genre, it is important to note that the two sections in vv. 2aβ + b and 3−9 are composed according to the traditional method by which case law corpora were composed, by moving from the common to the specific aspect(s). Furthermore, each of the two sections is composed according to the basic structure of case laws themselves, by an introductory protasis stating the case and a following apodosis stating the prescription for the case. Substantively, as well as syntactically, the two parts of each law belong together, and neither is isolated from the other.[12] And this is the point where the conceptual problems arise.

---

[12] The genre of case law in which this Yahweh instruction is cast means that an assumed genre "Ritual" consisting only of the texts contained in the apodoses (vv. 2b without 2aβ, and 3aβ−9 without 3aα, etc.) will not only have to be isolated from its extant redactional layers; it either will also have to be isolated from its case law protases in order to demonstrate an originally pure form of "Ritual," or its case law form will have to be included in the explanation of the form of a genre "Ritual." In any case, the relationship of case law and "Ritual," and the possible transformation of a purely prescriptive "Ritual" to case law will have to be explained.

§4 Style and theme in vv. 2aβ + b and 3−9

Stylistic observations have shown redactional influence in the combination of vv. 1 + 2aα, 2aβ + b, and 3 ff. This influence exists also in thematic respects. The main case law in v. 2aβ + b says essentially that a קרבן for Yahweh shall be brought from domestic animals,[13] i.e., "from the cattle and (not: "or") the small livestock." It raises the issue of the type of "offering," קרבן, with respect to the types of the materials to be used for it, and classifies the materials in a twofold manner.[14] However, instead of unfolding the two types of materials focused on in v. 2b, which is the thrust of the main case law, the rest of Lev 1, from v. 3 on, shifts to the aspect of the עלה, a subtype of קרבן, and subsequently subordinates the aspect of the materials in vv. 3−9, 10−13, 14−17 to the aspect of this sacrificial subtype. Vv. 3 ff. make it appear as if v. 2aβ + b had said: if anyone from among you brings a קרבן for Yahweh, you shall bring either an עלה or a מנחה or a זבח שלמים. That is not said, however. The shift in focus is not self-explanatory. The redactors could either have inserted a formulation in v. 2b like the one just indicated and thereby provided a thematically consistent introduction to the present macro-structure of Lev 1−3. Or they could have reorganized Lev 1−3 from 1:3 on, based on the subdivision of the sacrificial materials stated in v. 2b. After all, they must have reorganized materials at hand by splitting chapters 1 and 3. Either possibility shows that this conceptual shift, and the tension between 1:2b and 1:3 ff. resulting from it, is not necessary. But it also shows that the present organization of Lev 1−3, based on the types of sacrifices despite 1:2b, is for substantive reasons, and not only as a redaction historical phenomenon, more plausible than its reorganization under the influence of 1:2b. In confronting the relationship between the

---

[13] Reading according to the MT *atnach*.

[14] For the systematized references to species of animals and their assignment to certain types of sacrifices, cf. the commentaries and R. RENDTORFF (1967: 115−118, 148−149, 161−162, 228−230). K. ELLIGER says that this systematization was done by redaction (32). It is preferable to say that the redaction utilized an already existing traditional system of classified animals and their determination for sacrificial purposes.

types of sacrifices and the types of their materials and procedures, the texts are governed by the aspect of the types of sacrifices to which the aspect of their respective materials is subservient and by which the function and meaning of the texts are determined. This fact can even be observed in 1:2aβ + b where the reference to the types of sacrificial materials is a subordinate aspect to a type of sacrificial offering.[15]

It is clear that the conceptual tension between 1:2b and 1:3ff. is the result of the combination of the three sacrificial types of the קרבן with the classified sacrificial materials related to each of these types. But it is also clear that the text not only rests on conceptual distinctions but is also organized according to their priorities, resisting at least a major alternative possibility for its organization. We encounter the conceptual blueprint for the text, for its individuality, and not only what it says.

---

[15] The fact that the offering materials for the קרבן consist not only of animals is known. Cf. Lev 2, etc., and R. RENDTORFF (1967: 179−182). It also indicates once again the problematic nature of Lev 1:2b.

§5 Conceptual terminology

Attention must be paid to the relationship between the conceptual terminology in the text and the text's action-oriented language. Whereas the verbs in particular point to the main procedural activities, the nouns are conceptual signals which identify persons, places, and objects, especially the types of offerings and their respective sacrificial materials. Of the latter, קרבן and עלה refer wholistically to genres of offerings whose aspects include much more than the prescription of procedure alone.[16] They are especially operative in the text in the sense that the offerer is presumed to know what a קרבן and an עלה is in contradistinction to other sacrifices, and when and for what purpose one of them is advisable or due.[17] In addition to what the text says, it presupposes the conceptual knowledge of the types of offerings by the offerer. This presupposition is particularly operative in the protases which state what the offerer wants to do, whereas the apodoses determine how to do it.

These observations, which would have to be augmented, may help us to determine the relationship between the קרבן—עלה concept and the particular prescription of its procedure. The conceptual preunderstanding of the offering, of the cause for it, its type and intended effect, generates the need for the clarification of the stipulations for its appropriate performance. And the prescription of the procedure makes the actualization of this preunderstanding possible.

---

[16] In v. 6a, "he skins the עלה," is used for the material object, whereas in vv. 3aα and 9bβ it is used for the type of sacrifice.

[17] The modern exegete needs to learn what a קרבן, an עלה, etc., is, whereas the offerer of our text knows it in order to be able to discern what is due in a particular situation. For our exegetical knowledge of the sacrificial system cf., among others, J. MILGROM (1976); R. RENDTORF (1967). MILGROM, distinguishing between voluntary and mandatory offerings (1976: 764), counts those in Lev 1—3 among the voluntary ones. However, if the עלה expiates inadvertent transgressions of the individual, as MILGROM says (767, 769), one may have to qualify its "voluntary" nature: while expiation is necessary, the decision for it is voluntary.

Excursus: אדם *in Lev 1:2aβ*

It must be pointed out that the noun "'ādām, like nepeš, designates 'person', whether male or female" (Gruber: 39). The commentaries offer no explicit interpretation of this fact — as if the question if and to what extent women, either together with men or alone, were participating not only in the cult in general but especially in sacrifices, and how, were exegetically solved or hermeneutically irrelevant. In this regard, Gruber's observations are meritorious. Gruber's work is also significant for its comprehensive bibliographical references. The subject deserves an even more extensive treatment. A glance at the table of contents in R. Rendtorff's *Studien,* under the "Anlässe" sections for the עלה, reveals occasions such as: the daily *'ōlâ, 'ōlâ* as holiday and festival offering *(Feiertags- und Festopfer),* as king's offering *(Königsopfer),* and others such as: purification rites *(Reinigungsriten),* atonement *(Sühne),* recognition *(Anerkennung),* joy *(Freude),* thanksgiving *(Dank)* and the *'ōlâ* of the individual *(die 'ōlâ des Einzelnen).* With respect to the latter, Rendtorff (1967: 81−85) refers to the *'ōlâ* of a mother. In view of this scenario alone one would have to ask whether or not women participated in all these occasions, and if not in all, in which they did participate.

For our text, and for its related texts in the priestly writings, it is sufficient to state that the words אדם and נפש are gender-inclusive. They mean: either a man or a woman; a person, male or female. In the texts about sacrifice they refer to a sacrifice, or sacrifices brought by individuals, whereby the texts in Lev 1−3, in distinction to others, refer only to the types of sacrifice by those individuals but not to the occasions for them. Nor do those texts indicate if those "persons" consist of a certain class only, e.g., the commoners, or include the members of all classes of the society. Nevertheless, the scenario pointed out by Rendtorff demonstrates a broad range of access for women to the sacrificial cult in matters of individual cases. This access is cult-specific and is more than women's general participation in the variety of cultic events. And the nouns אדם and נפש are, again, examples of conceptual terminology which directly presuppose not only the writers' but also the readers' conscious awareness of their conceptuality and its self-evident implications for the sociology of the sacrificial cult. If anything should demonstrate the need in exegetical work not to overlook the explicit reconstruction of conceptual presuppositions operative in a text, this example alone would suffice.

Failure to reconstruct presuppositions leads either to making irrelevant that of which we are implicitly aware, or to excluding this exegetical issue outright. In either case the result of such exegetical work is the danger not only of an underdeveloped sociology of Israel, especially of its sacrificial system, but also of a one-sided perception of the implications of this specific factor for the exegesis of our, or any similar, pericope.

There are some open questions, however. While it is clear that אדם in 1:2aβ presupposes either a man or a woman, it is not equally clear that the text of vv. 3–9 presupposes the same alternative in its prescriptions for the actions of the offering persons. The text's prescriptions of the acts may or may not include women. Whichever is the case does not depend alone and automatically on the usage of the nouns אדם and נפש in the introductory statements of the cases. It is possible that the text presupposes an inclusive perspective in the noun while shifting away from it in its prescriptions. The problem cannot be pursued specifically at this juncture. Instead, the references used in Gruber's essay may serve as a case in point. They show that, among others, an עלה or חטאת is brought by a woman who also, if one follows the context, does the pressing of the hand down firmly and even the killing, so according to Lev 4:27–30, 32f., and the removing of the fat, Lev 4:35. All of these cases, however, involve animals from the "flock," צאן, whereas no "cattle," בקר, are involved. Also, Lev 12:6f., 14:12f., 15:29 say only, in language analogous to 1:3bα, that the person brings the animal to the entrance of the tent of meeting to the priest who then offers it before Yahweh. The questions are apparently: How far did the offerer's activity in the procedure go? Was there a difference in activity between men and women? And were men and women differently involved in different types of sacrifices and especially in different types of sacrificial materials? It may be more than coincidental that there is no textual evidence for women having to kill a steer or bull, בקר. But even such a restriction would appear to be a dispensation rather than a disqualification. In view of the fact that they could kill small livestock, צאן, it would point to the aspect of practicality rather than a reduction of women's qualification in sacrificial matters.

The question of women's involvement in sacrifices also has traditio-historical implications. One of these implications directly affects our text (Lev 1:3–9) and its related corpus. In their exegesis the commentaries not only say but also intend men as the ones referred to in vv. 3–9. Quite apart from this fact, the question arises whether this older text, without its late redactional expansion in vv. 1—2 which refers to אדם, did not indeed refer to male offerers only. If so, the extant redactional expansion would point to a significant *reconceptualization* in principle of the older prescription; if not, it would amount to a *recontextualization,* literally, by adding a context, which for necessary reasons made the traditional concept explicit. The answer to this question can only be given, if at all, in a circumspective traditio-historical investigation which will have to include the literary-historical assessment of the texts about ritual sacrifices in Leviticus.

For the time being, we will have to account for the possible conceptual tension between the reference to אדם in Lev 1:2 aβ and the persons, men only, presupposed in vv. 3—9. And while the assumption of women in vv. 3—9 cannot be excluded in principle — until we know better — the lack of evidence that women were ordered to kill cattle, בקר, causes us to assume that the actants meant in vv. 3—9 were specifically men, probably for practical reasons.

§6 The concept of the text, not of the performance

When speaking about the procedural actualization or implementation of the presupposed concept, a methodological *caveat* is in order. We speak about the writers' transformation of a concept into a text, not into an action, and interpret the concept of an observed text, not of an observed performance. Already the form of the case laws in vv. 2 aβ + b and 3−9, as well as the variability of the case law form in general, indicates that the text cannot *e silentio* be assumed to be a description or report about an actual ritual performance based on observation. Whatever our texts in vv. 2 aβ + b and 3−9 "describe," in its protasis as well as in its apodosis each of the two laws is prescriptive in the sense that in each both the case and the prescription for its actualization are considered as lying in the future. And the grammatical fact that the verb forms in the apodoses simply state actions does not mean that they have no prescriptive function.[18]

The assumption is legitimate that the depictions of the rituals in our texts reflect the *tradition* of sacrificial practices. This is supported by external evidence. This does not mean, however, that these texts represent narratives of observed actual performances.[19] Their prescriptive nature alone prohibits such conclusions, however much it presupposes the knowledge of ritual tradition. It may as well point to revised, reformatory, or new forms of procedure, an acute possibility if one allows for

---

[18] In other case laws, e.g., in the Covenant Book, the anticipated case (protasis) is described from the perspective of a future possibility which, when it occurs, will require its settlement which is prescribed in the apodosis. By contrast, the case anticipated in our text is described from the perspective of an action just happening, not yet having occurred as a *fait accompli,* for the simultaneous actualization of which the prescriptions are given.

[19] P. Rigby, e.g., asserts, "The postexilic cult of the second Temple was codified in the priestly tradition.... At this period of the Second Temple, Lv 1−7 was the regular and codified cult" (322). This one-sided assertion is unwarranted because it is not certain that the texts referred to represent the codification of the actual ritual performances already existing during the second temple period. And even if this were the case, the texts' own structures may be shaped by perspectives that differ from the perspectives derived from the observation of the actual ritual practice.

the historical origin of our texts in times of cultic controversy or of the demise of the sacrificial cult during the exile, and if one takes into account the fact that the agenda for rituals were not always the same in Israel's history.[20] We do not even know whether these laws were ever implemented as prescribed. And in as much as they were meant to be the basis for implementation, any comparison with what can be known about the situations at Sinai, from Sinai on, and at the first and second temple, will for various reasons keep the question open whether such implementation would have been in precise accordance with the prescriptions or whether descriptions or narratives about actual performances might have differed from the prescriptions before us in more or less significant respects.

These texts, therefore, cannot be interpreted by analogy to the method employed for reports or descriptions of observed ritual performances in anthropological field studies. This must be said quite apart from the necessary attention to the distinctions between ritual systems in different cultures and historical epochs, distinctions that forbid simplistic blanket applications of one ritual system for the interpretation of another. Compared with descriptions of observed rituals, the anthropological nature of our texts is not one of actual observation of performance, let alone of actual performance itself, but one of the *Geistesbeschäftigung* for – literally – a program, a *Vorschrift*. In what they express and presuppose, they are the results of this conceptualizing *Geistesbeschäftigung*. They reflect the system of this specific program even where this system is based on the tradition of actual procedures. This program may differ from the description of any observed performance, or of an entire system of performances. It must, therefore, be interpreted in its own right as a linguistically based expression and conceptuality of ritual reality.

---

[20] On these changes, cf. R. RENDTORFF (1967: especially 235–260). K. ELLIGER'S remark that innovations were hardly involved is not self-evident, particularly in view of some of his own interpretations concerning the change of the function of the עלה from an older *Hoheitsopfer* to *Sühnebeschaffung,* conerning the role of the lay person and the priest(s), concerning "dem kirchenpolitischen Einfluß," even redactionally in the text, of the Jerusalemite Aaronides in contrast to the traditions of other sanctuaries, concerning struggles for the admission to the priesthood in Jerusalem, concerning the history of the sacrificial practice, etc. (28–32).

Excursus: Ritual in anthropology, structuralism, and exegesis

A striking example of the misappropriation of ritual systems in interpretation would be the indiscriminate application of V. W. Turner's model of the ritual process as the conceptual framework for the interpretation of our texts. It would violate basic methodological rules for the exegesis of texts and for serious cross-cultural studies as well. Turner's illuminating interpretations of rituals among current African tribes (the Tallensi and Ashanti of Ghana, the Nuer of Sudan, et al.) reveal a basic hermeneutical framework within which these rituals operate. When applied to rituals of different cultures and times, including ancient Israel's, this framework will certainly elicit answers in response to what one looks for because classifications of life and death, paradoxes, models and processes of communities, and the liminality of status processes in humiliation and stratification are found everywhere. The following, however, are perfectly open questions: 1) whether or not this hermeneutical framework is in all societies and at all times of their history the same; 2) whether or not its elements are the only ones and have the same place and function in the system; and 3) whether distinctly different types of rituals from among many that exist in a society have their own specific hermeneutic, either based on the society's general framework or at variance with it.

Especially, however, Turner's interpretations are the result of field studies of actually observed ritual performances. His text describes and interprets those performances. But while a prescriptive text about a ritual will probably also reveal its hermeneutical system to a certain extent, it must not *e silentio* be presumed to be descriptive of actual performance, not only because there is − as in our biblical texts − no evidence for it but also because even such description represents an interpretive distancing *vis-à-vis* the performance. Turner himself is perfectly aware of this fact when, after quoting the interpreting comments made by a member of the Ndembu tribe on a just-performed ritual (86−88) he says: "But, naturally, it [this account] leaves out many of those fascinating details that for the anthropologists constitute the major clues to a culture's private universe" (88).

Of course, nothing is said against the validity of Turner's own interpretations, or against the results of anthropological field studies on ritual. What is instead emphasized is that 1) the prescription of a ritual in a text is not identical with the description of an observed ritual, let alone with a performed ritual itself; 2) that a hermeneutical system or a "culture's private universe" of ritual is not everywhere and at all times the same; and 3) that different types of rituals have their respectively different systems and significance. It is especially emphasized that each specific system must be investigated on its own specific terms, by way of a heuristic procedure which attempts to discover it inductively, rather than by the imposition of a preconceived set of questions taken from outside, be those questions transcultural or ritual-specific. Such imposition will yield results to the extent to which a specific ritual system responds to the questions asked of it, but without necessarily revealing its own identity. It may well obscure or even destroy that identity. It certainly does not reveal a text's individuality.

The present study of the relationship between the text and its concept must also be distinguished from attempts at discovering patterns by way of the structuralist method in as much as this method focuses on unconscious structures. The study by P. Rigby, "A Structural Analysis of Israelite Sacrifice and Its Other Institutions," claims to have this aim. Rigby endeavors to understand "the unconscious of the Israelite mind" (299), "to grasp the unconscious structure underlying the institution of Israelite sacrifice" (302, 303), its unconsciously "operative mind-set," or "'grammar'" (303). He adopts Levi-Strauss's definition which says that structuralism "goes from the study of the conscious content to that of unconscious forms [...] seeking to attain, through the conscious [...] more and more of the unconscious" (299–300).

It should be admitted that the search for the level of the unconscious is legitimate also in the Old Testament literature. However, it is doubtful if any of Rigby's arguments demonstrate evidence for that level.

His quotation of Levi-Strauss just referred to does not mean that the "unconscious forms" are the only alternative to "the conscious content." Forms or, as in our case, concepts – a word also used by Rigby (305, 308, etc.) – are not only unconscious, they may be conscious, and very often are. The fact that concepts are often unexplicated, unexpressed, unsaid in a text does not mean that they are unconscious. These distinctions between conscious and unconscious concepts equally unexpressed in texts, and the criteria for them, are important. Yet they are discussed neither in his methodological statements nor in his material on the holocaust and the aspects related to it (311–328), material that is specifically pertinent for the present study.

Consequently, no evidence is established in Rigby's material discussion as to what is conceptually conscious or unconscious. It may be more than coincidental that the word "unconscious" occurs only in his methodological statements (299−303, 309) and at the end of his treatment of the holocaust under the rubric of "The Foundation Structure" (328), but not in his discussion of the materials said to reveal that structure (311−327). One wonders why "Israel's mind-set" (307), "the fundamental concepts of Israel's society" (308), the concepts of "equilibrium" (308, 312), and of "normality" (306) rather than of "neutrality" (312), of "normal life" (312), of the holy land (313), the theocratic institutions (313) of covenant (318, 323) and holy war (314) and of the structure of the holocaust, and the interdependence of them all, should be considered *a priori* as being based on the unconscious.

Why should Rigby's structural presentation of his "Foundation Structure" (312), which he assumes to reflect the basic structure of the holocaust, point to the level of the unconscious? The offerer brings the עלה because he/she knows about the equilibrium and that it is disturbed by Yahweh's threat. He/she may also know the reason for the disturbance. If not, he/she is at worst unconscious of the *reasons* but at the same time very conscious of the disturbance itself. It is the disturbance, however, and the consciousness of it as upsetting the equilibrium of normal life, that prompts the gift of the עלה. The basis for the conscious structure of the עלה is the consciously structured experience of the disturbance of the equilibrium and of the need for overcoming it. Of course, exegetically it must be said that Rigby's classification of the holocaust under his "Foundation Structure" fails to take into account that the עלה was not only given in reaction to a threat by Yahweh but also in grateful response to the just-experienced removal of such a threat by Yahweh's gift of new grace or to nothing but a received blessing or salvation in the first place.

It may be that for Rigby, the unconscious stands for the mind of Yahweh which is revealed in "a theophany" (312, etc.). Apart from such an extremely problematic identification of the unconscious with Yahweh's mind, it must be said that once Yahweh's mind-set is theophanically revealed, it no longer belongs to the unconscious mind-set of Israel. What is revealed is conscious. As far as the "Foundation Structure" of the holocaust is assumed to be caused by revelation, it exists in a state of human consciousness, and the conscious structures of Israel's institutions are the actualizations of its conscious perceptions of reality.

Indeed, Rigby's entire discussion of the biblical texts and concepts (311–328) evokes the impression that the texts demonstrate a high degree of consciousness of the unexplicated structures or concepts operative in them. That these presupposed concepts are by and large not contained or explained in separate systematic and theoretical treatises, and must be reconstructed from occasional *intra-textual* signals, text-structures, and by *con-* and *inter-* textual exegesis, as is often done, has nothing to do with an *a priori* assumption of their unconscious nature. Our discussion will, therefore, have to focus first of all on the distinction between the explicit text and the inexplicit concept operative in the text. And only under the reconstruction of inexplicit concepts or structures will the question arise whether or not what is presupposed without being said belongs to Israel's conscious conceptualities or to the level of the unconscious.

§7 The issue of presuppositions

Before discussing the text and concept of Lev 1:3−9 we will have to address the issue of presuppositions. On our text, as everywhere else, the commentaries refer to the aspect of inexplicit presuppositions randomly rather than systematically, and especially without distinguishing between their different functions. Examples must suffice.

K. Elliger says that this text does not explain the word תמים in v. 3aβ because such an explanation − which is found in Lev 22:22−24 − "liegt nicht im Plan der Niederschrift," which was interested in something else (*Leviticus,* 34). R. Rendtorff argues similarly when saying that בן בקר in v. 5 does not refer to the age of the bull because "einerseits vermeidet dieses Ritual gerade die Festlegung und beschreibt nur, was zu geschehen hat.... andererseits käme eine Altersbestimmung hier verspätet ..." (*Leviticus,* 50). In both examples, the silence of the text on what it does or may not presuppose is explained with reference to its own plan, interest, intention, or to contextual suitability. However, these legitimate references do not mean that what is presupposed in the text is therefore irrelevant for it. Indeed, those inexplicit presuppositions may be very relevant assumptions for the prescribed performance. The text's silence about the meaning of תמים (*heil,* complete) means only that it emphasizes the activities. But it assumes at the same time that the lay person knows the kind of bull that meets the prescribed criteria when selecting it. The text assumes such knowledge, and this assumption is operative in its conceptuality just as much as in the lay person's activities themselves, or else the "plan" of the text cannot be implemented legitimately in this case. Also, it is true that בן בקר in v. 5a refers to the "individual" animal in a descriptive *(beschreibend)* sense, especially as long as one presumes an original unit consisting of vv. 4−9 only. In a unit vv. 3−9, however, this description presupposes a concomitant understanding of the qualifications of the animal − "male and perfect" − already expressed in v. 3aβ. The "described" animal in v. 5a is not just any "individual bull," even in an older unit. Even its mere description presupposes the discerning knowledge of its qualifications on the part of the offerer.[21]

M. Noth says that the utilization or disposal of the animal's skin is perhaps "stillschweigend vorausgesetzt" (1962: 13). Unless "still-schweigend" is a truism for any inexplicit presupposition, it may mean that what is presupposed is not said although it is positively assumed to be known. *Caveat:* In the realm of assumed knowledge as well as in the realm of prescribed actions, not everything is equally important. The value of a "perfect" bull is different from the value of its skin and its utilization. In either case, the presupposed but positively assumed knowledge is part of the conceptuality of the text, of its vision of the total action-process, and of its criteria for what it says. The exegetical reconstruction of this conceptuality is important, if for no other reason than to clarify what the lay person needs to learn through the prescriptions in comparison with what he is presumed already to know – should the prescriptions intend to instruct him.

In view of what has been said, K. Elliger's formulations that the lay person "weiss Bescheid" about the skinning and dissection of the animal, that this knowledge "wird vorausgesetzt und interessiert jedenfalls nicht" (35) is one-sided. Cf. also M. Noth (1962: 13), followed by R. Rendtorff (1985: 49): it is not the "Aufgabe des Rituals." For his performance, the offerer's knowledge is certainly of interest. True, to express this presupposition is not the task of the prescriptions proper. But what is the difference between the offerer's presupposed knowledge about how to dispense with the animal, and the prescriptions? Why is said what is said, and why not what is not said? What does the text itself presuppose for what needs to be said and what need not be said? What is the criterion for this difference? As for the offerer, who is assumed to know all the unsaid things, why is he not assumed to know also the most elementary of all? Does he really have to be instructed about the most basic actions, the most self-explanatory ones, if there is no need for instructing him about at least some important details of which he may not be aware? Is the text lay instruction? Or

---

[21] בן בקר refers to the "individual" exemplar of the species. However, for expressions of the individual exemplar of the species בקר alone, the priestly terminology, too, used the words שׁור = a grown steer, and פר (בן) = young steer. One will have to qualify this: בן בקר in Lev 1:5a can refer to the individual exemplar and to nothing else only if the relative age of the animal did not matter in this text – which may or may not be the case.

would a comparison between the inexplicit and the explicit, rather than the declaration of the text's "disinterest" in the inexplicit, point to a possibly different intention or function of the text?

Indeed, the commentaries abound with observations that explain the texts themselves with reference to their inexplicit presuppositions. E.g., K. Elliger speaks about "die Abgrenzung der Tätigkeit von Priestern und Laien" (34); that the lay person has to work with the priest "Hand in Hand" (31, 34): while (!) the priest sprinkles the blood, the offerer skins the animal (35); after (!) the blood-rite, the priest prepares the fire (35); while (!) the priest puts the pieces onto the fire, the offerer "unterdessen" washes the intestines (35), and so on. The aspect of "Abgrenzung" is documented reasonably clearly by the text, but the aspect of simultaneous or successive (inter)action is derived from the exegesis of what the text presupposes without saying so. The exegesis of these inexplicit presuppositions of the text is so important for Elliger that he sees in them the very blueprint for the text itself, "den Plan der Niederschrift, der es vielmehr" − in contradistinction to other presuppositions that were not part of that blueprint! − "auf die rechte Verteilung der anfallenden Arbeiten ankommt" (34).

It is problematic when the exegete dismisses the interpretation of one inexplicit presupposition in a text while placing a high priority on another one. Such judgments demonstrate that presuppositions are not irrelevant for or inoperative in the text because they are inexplicit. They rest instead on the exegete's differentiation between those presuppositions that belong to the plan of the text and those that do not. That differentiation, however, rests on the exegetical reconstruction of a certain plan, a reconstruction that may be right or wrong. When saying that the plan of our text aims at the instruction of the lay person about his interaction with the priest, Elliger interprets not only explicit signals of the text. Instead, he interprets the implicit assumptions of the text, assumptions to be known and understood, or at least the relationship between the statements of the text, which are merely listed successively, without which the text itself and its instructing intention cannot be understood. The sentences of the text are simply connected by *waw* 's, but it is clear, and has been correctly observed, that the sequence of the connected sentences does not correspond to the presupposed sequence or the order of the prescribed actions. Nor do the perfect or imperfect forms of the verbs indicate such a sequence. Because of this point, the import of exegetically assumed presuppositions of the text affects the translation of the text. G. J. Wenham, e.g., translates: v. 4a + b = "then" − "so that"; v. 5a + b = "then" − "and"; v. 6a + b = "then" − "and"; v. 7 = "then" (!); v. 8 = "and"; v. 9a + b = "but" − "and" (48). Whether correct or not, these translations are based on interpretation of the text's inexplicit presuppositions as much as on grammar.

For the transition from v. 6 to v. 7, M. Noth says that after the lay person has skinned and dissected the animal, "nunmehr ist wieder der Priester an der Reihe" (1962: 13), which is an interpretation of the assumed presupposition of the text but not of what it actually says. Is it the priest's turn after the offerer's action because v. 7 follows v. 6 and because of consecutive *waw*'s? Other examples could be given.

On another point, R. Rendtorff emphasizes the number of the ritual acts proper which basically follow one another (1985: 32, 48, 50, 54, 55, 57, 60). He distinguishes between *Nebenhandlungen* in vv. 7 and 9a and the sacrificial acts proper, among others in vv. 6a + b and 8, and refers to the discrepancy between the sequence in the text's prescriptions and in the sacrificial performance (55, 57, 59). But he does not focus on the aspect of simultaneous or successive actions presupposed in the text, apparently because the text is interested in "den konkreten Einzelheiten des Opfervollzugs," in "was zu geschehen hat" (20) in "den Ablauf der Opferhandlung Schritt für Schritt festzuhalten," in its exact description (18) of "dem richtigen Vollzug" (62). True, the text for the most part successively prescribes a series of concrete actions for a particular עלה. But does it prescribe what has to happen "exactly," "step by step," in its *Einzelheiten?* Would not such interest in exactness and detail also have to express most of the details of each action that are only *e silentio* positively presupposed? Why are some actions expressed but most of their details *(Einzelheiten)* and additional actions are not? For a different perspective, cf. M. Noth's "sehr einfache, fast eintönige Aneinanderreihung" (1962: 10); and K. Elliger's remark that the work "ist nur in großen Zügen beschrieben" (34). And if by "der Ablauf," the flow and correct execution of the sacrificial procedure should be meant, does not this aspect point to the interdependence of the acts in the procedural system rather than to the exact acts, and therefore also to the aspect of the simultaneous and successive interaction of the involved persons, at their respective places? If "step by step" refers not only to each specific step but also to their systemic connectedness, what is the uniqueness of this עלה system that generates the order of these steps? Which actions are constitutive for that system, and how many? Rendtorff lists for vv.

4−9 ten acts (1985: 18), based on the perf. forms, which excludes v. 9a on grammatical-syntactical and substantive grounds ("Nebenhand-lung"; 1985: 59). He lists seven sacrificial acts (1985: 32−60), thereby eliminating the *Nebenhandlungen* in vv. 5b, 7a + b (1985: 55, 57−59). His criterion for seven acts is the judgment about the ritual acts proper, a judgment apparently based on his conclusion that this and its related texts belong to the genre "Ritual" (1985: 19). However, this judgment rests on the exegetical reconstruction of the system of a prescriptive genre which agrees neither with the surface-structure of the text nor with the number of actions envisioned for its performance. The identification of the ritual proper ("das eigentliche Ritual"; 1985: 32) and its seven steps from among ten or eleven listed in the text might be legitimate. But it is an abstraction from the text and from the presuppositions that generated at least its individuality. It could only be understood as a generic nucleus out of which the text was formed on presuppositions of its own. What is constitutive for the text, for its ten steps if one accounts for vv. 5b, 7a + b, or for its eleven or twelve or thirteen steps if one also accounts for vv. 3a + b, 9a? This question is not yet explained with reference to the well-known argument that generic patterns are adapt-able to variations in individual texts. What is it that causes those varia-tions, even if they should confirm the identified genre rather than point to a different one? The exegetical distinction between "ritual proper" and *Nebenhandlungen* obviously serves to identify those acts that are qualitatively essential, decisive, constitutive for the correct, legitimate execution ("den richtigen Vollzug"), of the ritual (Rendtorff, 1985: 62). But if the text is instruction for such correct and legitimate execution, for which the seven steps of the ritual proper would have to be critically distinguished from the side-actions, why does the text also, and indis-criminately, mention those side-actions? Even if it would, or were to, presuppose that the actants knew this important difference automatical-ly, why does the text blur it by adding acts that do note belong to the ritual proper? What are the presuppositions operating in the text that generated the combination of the ritual proper and its secondary or accessory actions? Or to what extent does the text presuppose such a distinction? What is the concept of this text? The reference to the seven actions proper is not a sufficient answer to these questions.

G. J. Wenham adds another dimension of presuppositions not explicit in the text. He refers to additional components: "It is very unlikely that it" − the laying on of hand − "was done all in silence. Most probably the

worshipper explained at this point why he was bringing the sacrifice.....
Certainly the priest must also have said something to assure the worshipper ..." (53). These and similar aspects are valuable for a synopsis of the
total sacrificial system. But they only provoke the question why no
reference is made in the text to such word-events. The prescribed ritual
is a speechless one. Of course, we do not know at all if the actions of each
and every sacrificial ritual were − supposed to be − accompanied by
verbal declarations, and if so, at what point before or during the procedure they were spoken. Had the text prescribed or even quoted a
declaration accompanying the act of pressing the hand down firmly, we
would probably have no problems understanding the meaning of that
act.

At any rate, if the text presupposes spoken words, this presupposition
is not operative in the text and plays no role in its concept. In fact, its
inexplicitness would point to the possibility of a split between action and
word in the concept fo this ritual, an assumption difficult to rationalize;
and if not a split, then to a serious default by not prescribing an essential
component of the ritual procedure for the instruction of the offerer −
should such instruction be intended. Our text is certainly not an instruction about the entire עלה system. Conceptually, it presupposes, focuses
on, and speaks only about one aspect of this system. Why this is so,
Wenham does not explain. He comes close to the problem when saying
that "because they understood the purpose of the burnt offering so well,
the men of ancient Israel have left this most common OT sacrifice largely
without explanation" (55). This is correct. It may not have been their
problem, but it is ours, or else we do not understand what they did and
understood themselves to be doing, and why their texts express what
they express and nothing else. Their understanding itself of what they
were doing and expressing is part of the concept of the text. It is an
intrinsic element of the text's anthropology.

§8 Lev 1:3−9. The relationship of protasis and apodosis

We must now focus on the relationship between text and concept in Lev 1:3−9. These verses represent above all a subordinate case law unit, with the protasis in v. 3aα and the apodosis in vv. 3aβ−9. The inquiry should, therefore, proceed first of all on the basis of the two subdivisions of this unit. Specifically, it should consider the second subdivision in its entirety, from v. 3aβ rather than only from v. 4 on, and explain the whole of the apodosis in relationship to its protasis.

The formulation of the protasis in v. 3aα, אם־עלה קרבנו מן־הבקר, anticipates a case in which "his gift from the cattle" will be an עלה, a burnt offering. This formulation is generated by a number of aspects which add up to the offerer's presupposed conceptual knowledge of what he is going to do. He must know that he is in a life situation that causes the advisability or need for an offering "for Yahweh." He must know that this particular situation has something to do with Yahweh, and that an offering is the link between his situation and Yahweh. He must also know that his offering, his gift, קרבן, is an עלה, a whole or burnt offering, a specific subtype of קרבן, which presupposes his knowledge not only of those subtypes themselves but also of their purpose. Regardless whence he has this knowledge, our law presupposes it although it does not explicate it − which it could have done and which is done in other instances.

Was that sort of knowledge among lay persons assumed to be automatic or the result of an educational system? Of course, the offerer is presumed to be familiar, probably automatically, with the classified typology of animals such as wild and domestic ones, cattle and their subtypes, small livestock and its subtypes, and (domestic!) "birds," v. 14, but also − automatically or through education? − with the either cultic or economic reasons for offering a particular type of animal such as an exemplar from cattle rather than from other possible subtypes. We have not even mentioned the difference between clean and unclean animals. He must be cognizant of the relationship between the type of offering and the offering material, i.e., that the material serves the עלה

offering and the offering material, i.e., that the material serves the עלה and its function rather than vice versa. Last but by no means least, he must be aware of the relationship between the עלה and himself: that the case focuses on his עלה − offering/gift from the cattle, and not on himself. Although he, together with the priest(s), is the grammatical subject in the following apodosis, he himself is subject to his עלה. What happens to the עלה animal in the prescribed activities?

All this presupposed knowledge amounts to a fairly sophisticated perception by lay people in which discerned factors such as personal life situations, their religious and cultic implications, sacrificial classifications as well as those of animals, together with their purposes, coincide. One wonders about the sociological nature of such a picture. This presupposed knowledge is both the cause for and the implication of the case stated in v. 3aα. Without it, there would be no case, let alone a prescription for its solution. And the actual offering, together with this knowledge of the case, represents the concern to which the following apodosis in vv. 3aβ−9, the prescription proper, responds.

For the relationship of v. 3aα and vv. 3aβ−9, another observation may be of some relevance. V. 3aα is a subordinated nominal clause, whereas the following main unit consists of verb clauses, save vv. 3bβ and 9bβ. The prescriptions refer to a series of actions, whereas the statement about the case refers to an existing state or condition or presupposition calling for these actions. The questions arises whether this existing state is considered only as applying to the duration of the actions prescribed in the apodosis or also to the situation in which the decision about his עלה gift from the cattle is made, before the series of actions begins. The latter understanding would mean that the protasis and the apodosis are related in the sense that the protasis expresses the side of the theoretically conceptualized plan and decision, whereas the apodosis expresses the side of the practical execution of that plan. There are indicators which support this understanding.

§9 The apodosis in 1:3 aβ—bα

The prescription proper belongs to a subgenre of case law, to procedural law. It focuses on procedure. It begins in v. 3aβ, regardless whether v. 3aβ + bα belongs to the "ritual proper" or not. Vv. 3aβ and bα consist of two prescriptions (in imperf. verb forms). They are united in a synthetic parallelism which indicates both a common perspective and a differentiation. Specifically, they refer not only to two different aspects of the same action of the offerer concerning the animal: יקריבנו / יקריב אתו, but also to the consecutive order of these two aspects in the same action: he shall bring it זכר תמים, and אל־פתח אהל מועד. The sequential order of the two statements is scarcely coincidental or a matter of indifference.

The question arises whether the action required in vv. 3aβ and bα is meant as a general introduction to vv. 4—9, as their *logical* presupposition, or as the first steps of the entire procedure which precede the rest in chronological order; in other words, whether the verb יקריב with object refers, inclusively, to the total process of the עלה sacrifice, or to particular steps in it. The commentaries focus, justifiably but exclusively, on the qualifications of the animal and on the place to which it must be brought. In the pericope itself, however, it is also twice said that he must *bring* the animal.

That the offerer must bring a "male, perfect" animal presupposes not only that he knows the difference between male and female, and perfect and imperfect exemplars of cattle,[22] but also that he selects from among his cattle (it is "his gift" from his property) one exemplar, at home, before he brings it to the sanctuary. This is all preliminary to what can be done with the animal as required from v. 4 on. The sequence of the stages

---

[22] K. ELLIGER is stating the obvious when stating that the word תמים, which is explained in Lev 22:22—24, is not explained in our text because such an explanation "liegt nicht im Plan der Niederschrift" (34). But why does it not belong to this plan? We may qualify this: תמים is not explained at this juncture because the offerer is presumed to know the criteria for it himself, and not because Lev 22:22—24, or a priest for that matter, teaches him thus as he selects the animal.

in 3 aβ–bα is considered, and not reversible. The text operates on the conceptual presupposition of a process which distinguishes between the offerer's previous involvement with the עלה=bull, and his involvement with the procedure for it at the sanctuary. The process begins with the decision and plan for בקר=עלה, v. 3 aα, itself caused by a particular life situation. And the prescription for the first stage envisions the activities of the lay person as setting in already at his home place, as involving the selection of the proper animal from his own cattle (or purchased from someone else's?) and, literally, as getting on the way and bringing it אל־פתח אהל מועד, to the tent of meeting. This part of the prescribed procedure distinctly precedes the following part from v. 4 on, regardless of where the "ritual proper" of that part is thought to begin. It belongs to the text's procedural prescription, for good reasons. Neither his pilgrimage to the sanctuary nor his planned slaughter of the animal is considered a secular act. Both must be seen on the background of the tradition of pilgrimages of individuals to the sancturary.[23]

The expression אל־פתח, v. 3 bα, refers to a particular spot in the priestly vision of the layout of the sanctuary. For diagrams see K. Koch and B. Reicke (1966: 1875–76, with further literature); G. J. Wenham (531). J. Milgrom (1970: 17–18), followed by R. Rendtorff (1985: 30) defines פתח as the "corridor within the sanctuary enclosure ... which extended between the enclosure gate and the courtyard altar."[24] It is clear that he is to bring the animal to the area before the tent. It is not quite clear precisely where the firm pressing down of the hand, v. 4a, and the slaughter, v. 5a, are to take place, and whether both actions happen at the same spot. Lev 1:11 specifically identifies the spot of slaughter as "on the north side of the altar," about 25 cubits away from the door of the enclosure. One may assume with Wenham (53) that the location for the act of pressing down the hand was not, at least not

---

[23] The priestly text claims only one legitimate sanctuary: the "tent of meeting," or "tabernacle," or "sanctuary" which is established and around which the tribes are organized thereafter. It is not in the center of the camp, but its place constitutes the center for the camp. More to the point: in the Pentateuchal tradition, this concept of the sanctuary has replaced the other, older tradition of the location of the ark outside the camp. On the *"Ohel Moed Konzeption,"* cf. now H. UTZSCHNEIDER (127); J. MILGROM (1990: 12, 17–18).

[24] For the discussion on פתח אהל מועד cf. also, among others: BARTELMUS (847–48); H. UTZSCHNEIDER (125–127). There is reason for assuming that the expression פתח אהל מועד is not always seen as referring to the total realm between the enclosure gate and the altar. It may on occasion refer to particular spots within that realm, even to the entrance to the tent itself.

necessarily, identical with the location for the animal's slaughter. It may be thought of, so Wenham, as happening at the door of the enclosure while the offerer entered through the door, after which and whence he proceeded to the place of slaughter. While not conclusive, this possibility has some support in the text.

§ 10 The firm pressing down of the hand,[25] Lev 1:4

From v. 4 on, the actions at the tent of meeting are prescribed. Clearly, the offerer is to press his hand down firmly on the animal's head before he kills it. Also, the pressing down of the hand must be considered as a separate act rather than as a mechanism in the animal's slaughter. Cf. R. Rendtorff (1985: 48) following B. Janowski (219). This understanding is supported by the position of v. 4b – לו לכפר עליו ונרצה – between vv. 4a and 5a. V. 4b specifically interprets the act of pressing the hand down prescribed in v. 4a, and not the act of slaughter prescribed in v. 5a of which the pressing of the hand would be a supporting part. It presupposes that the hand is pressed down on the animal's head while the animal is still alive and before it is killed. Because this act with its specific meaning takes place before the killing, it may well be considered to take place at the door of the enclosure, at the moment of entering it, whence it is led to the specific place of slaughter. If this view is defensible, it would mean that the text presupposes the continuation of the process of steps from v. 3aβ on: the offerer selects the bull, brings it to the entrance of the tent where, specifically at entering the enclosure gate, he puts his hand on its head, whence he proceeds to the place of slaughter. But the alternative must be left open that he is to proceed to the place of slaughter directly where both actions take place, consecutively but separately.

The flow of the prescriptions from v. 3aβ on, which points to the understanding of a process of consecutive actions, is interrupted the first time by the clause לרצנו לפני יהוה in v. 3bβ: "for/to the (purpose – or effect – of) favor to him before Yahweh."[26] R. Rendtorff (1985: 30–32)

---

[25] It is better to translate סמך, v. 4a, with "press down firmly" than with "lay," as is frequently done in English translations, such as WENHAM's (48). The meaning of this act is most probably different from what is generally understood by "laying on of hands" – whatever that is interpreted to mean.

[26] The verb רצה means "etwas gut finden, Gefallen haben an etwas"; its abstract noun רצון mostly expresses "die subjektive Empfindung des Wohlgefallens, d.h. der Huld und Gnade eines Höhergestellten bzw. Gottes," G. GERLEMAN (811). English translations normally say "accept," e.g., *RSV,* and G. J. WENHAM's "so that the LORD may accept

has acutely argued that the two elements of this clause, לרצנו and לפני יהוה, refer, each respectively, to the two preceding prescriptions, and concluded: "Zwei Aspekte werden damit betont: 1. Das Opfer muß einwandfrei beschaffen sein, damit es dem Opfernden zum <Wohlgefallen> dienen kann.... 2. Das Opfertier muß an den richtigen Ort gebracht werden, damit es <vor Jahweh> dargebracht werden kann" (31–32). Of course, when interpreting ונרצה לו, the first half of the second interpretive statement in v. 4b(α), Rendtorff also says that indispensable for ונרצה לו, "and it will be granted to him favourably," is the pressing down of the hand; and he adds, following the rabbinic tradition, that this firm pressing is the only act for which the offerer cannot be replaced (35–36). It is not quite clear whether v. 4b(α) refers to the עלה only, the grammatical object of סמך in v. 4a, as Rendtorff says (36), or to the entire sentence, v. 4a, especially to the act itself of firmly pressing the hand downward. It is likewise unclear when, how, and possibly where it happens that "it will be granted to him favourably."

Unless we presume that the two interpretive statements in vv. 3bβ and 4b(α) have been placed indiscriminately and have remained so even though their place might be the result of a redactional accident, we should interpret them in light of their place in their context. In this context, and only here in our passage, the issue of what is or happens in the offerer's favor is connected with two specific actions among all of those in the procedure: with his having brought the correctly selected animal — is its correctness and maleness checked and approved? — and his firm placing of his hand on the animal. Whether or not what the offerer does amounts to favor for him depends on and is limited in this text to these two actions.[27] These judgements in his favor appear to be

---

him" (48). B. A. LEVINE translates: "for acceptance in his behalf before the LORD" (5). The translation using "accept, acceptance" is not satisfactory. It misses a particular emphasis. One may have to accept something or somebody even though one does not like it. The Hebrew word highlights pleasure, agreement, and favor, whereas "acceptance" may be a connotation depending on the favorable response by someone who "accepts" someone else's approach or gift. I prefer on these grounds the traditional German translations, e.g., R. RENDTORFF's "ihm zum Wohlgefallen vor Jahweh" and on v. 4bα "so wird ihm Wohlgefallen zuteil" (1985: 15).

[27] N. KIUCHI argues, with good observations on the connection of רצון in v. 3bβ with נרצה in v. 4bα, that the "sacrifice" is brought *"for* acceptance" and that this pupose is accomplished when the sacrifice is "accepted" following the firm pressing down of the hand (117). This exegesis is possible. It amounts to the "acceptance" of one act only, the act of pressing the hand down firmly, rather than of two acts as in my own argument. In either case, what is called "acceptance" is confined to what is said to happen before vv. 5–9, and

presuppositions for the following actions in v. 5 on rather than dependent on them. It seems that conceptually v. 4 belongs in the prescribed process closer to v. 3 than is generally assumed, regardless of the question of where the "ritual proper" begins and despite the text's differentiation between the procedure preceding the arrival at the sanctuary and the procedure at the sanctuary itself.[28]

This means, first of all, that vv. 3—4 focus on what is to the offerer's own favor, whereas vv. 5—9 do not presuppose this aspect but end up instead, in v. 9b, the third interpretive statement of the text, which says what is in Yahweh's interest in the procedure. It is to the offerer's favor that his two identified acts are met with positive, delighted approval, apparently as a precondition for what follows. It means further that the text distinguishes between two procedural stages at the sanctuary, one for the living and, subsequently, another for the dead עלה animal. The aspect of the animal's transition from its life to its death in the sacrificial concept also presupposes its transition from the offerer's to Yahweh's property, "before Yahweh" (לפני יהוה) vv. 3bβ—5a, and "for Yahweh" (ליהוה) v. 9bβ. As long as the animal is alive, it may be selected and dedicated for an עלה, but it is still the offerer's animal. Once the עלה animal is ritually killed, it belongs to Yahweh, v. 9bβ. The procedural prescription presupposes this transition.

What, then, does v. 4a, the prescription of the firm pressing down of the hand, mean?[29] V. 4b explains only its concomitant result and the purpose of that result,[30] but the act itself of pressing down is nowhere explained.[31] Is the explanation absent because the text — and the antici-

---

does not cover the total procedure which KIUCHI seems to assume. His interpretation of one accepted act rests on the correlation of a statement of purpose with the statement of its actualization, in isolation, however, from the syntactical connection of each of these clauses from its main clause and also in isolation from their respectively different subsequent qualifications: לפני יהוה in v. 3bβ², and לכפר עליו in v. 4bβ. These factors give cause to assume two actions or stages expressed in the two main clauses in vv. 3 and 4 for which the offerer needs and/or receives favor.

[28] This interpretation implies also that the favor granted the offerer for these two actions does not refer to his life situation which causes him to bring an עלה.

[29] For the comprehensive discussion cf., among others, WRIGHT/MILGROM/FABRY (880—89); R. RENDTORFF (1985: 32—48); F. STOLZ ("*smk* stützen," 1976: 160—162); B. JANOWSKI (199—221); N. KIUCHI (112—119).

[30] For v. 4bβ see below.

[31] We would be better off had the text reported what G. J. WENHAM assumes: "most probably the worshipper explained at this point why he was bringing the sacrifice" (53). Did he also speak a formula that defined *what* he was doing?

pated worshipper — presupposes its knowledge or because the act "wäre gedankenlos im Zug der Systematisierung eingetragen worden,"[32] without an understanding of its meaning? Again, we may exegetically be disinterested in what the text does not say. But quite apart from the extensive scholarly discussion of and interest in this question, such disinterest in what the text presupposes would certainly affect our exegesis of the anthropology and theology of the text, i.e., of whether or not it understood the nature of its prescription and presumed the worshipper to understand what he was supposed to do. What the text does not explain is still necessary for us to know.

The act has been said to effect the transfer of sin from the offerer to the animal,[33] to symbolize the identification of offerer and animal so that the animal's death substitutes for the offerer's death, and to symbolize the offerer's right of property, his *Besitzrecht*.[34] R. Rendtorff concludes his extensive discussion saying that "Völlige Klarheit läßt sich in dieser Frage jedoch nicht gewinnen" (1985: 48).[35] We may consider another possibility.

Thus far we have argued for a level of conceptual coherence of vv. 3–4 *vis-à-vis* vv. 5–9. In all priestly sacrificial texts the firm pressing down of the hand immediately precedes the killing of the animal.[36] It happens on the living animal. It is not a subsidiary component of the animal's killing.

---

[32] R. RENDTORFF (1985: 43).

[33] In addition to RENDTORFF's rejection of this argument (1985: 41) one has to ask why anything at all should be transferred if an קרבן – עלה presupposes no sin.

[34] So typically J. PEDERSEN (366); quoted by RENDTORFF: "By this act he establishes the fact that the animal is his property" (1985: 44). But why should he establish this fact with this act if, as the text says, the offerer brings *his* gift which must have been recognized as such upon entering the court before he presses his hand down upon the animal's head? Or should we assume that the text presupposes that the offerer when appearing with his animal had first of all to answer the question whether it is his property (bought or chosen from his own stock) or whether he stole it? Even so, would the answer to such a question not be a simple yes or no rather than a specific ritual action, to be given at entering the precincts rather than as part of the ritual? It seems that the meaning of the act points in the opposite direction.

[35] N. KIUCHI, while also stating the lack of scholarly consensus (112) and referring to a five-fold typology of potential meanings of the act of pressing the hand down firmly established by A. M. RODRIGUEZ says in his own conclusion that this act "in Lev 1:4 simply expresses the idea of substitution" (117; also 119, 141). But the fact that this act "will be accepted on *his* behalf" does not necessitate the conclusion that "on *his* behalf" — which is already an interpretive translation of לו anyway — qualifies the act of pressing down as substitution. If that were so, the exegetical crux should not have existed.

[36] See R. RENDTORFF (1985: 32–35).

Nor is it connected with the blood-rite,[37] and has no atoning function in the עלה ritual.[38] It is one of two actions before the killing for which the offerer receives רצון, favor. Its position immediately before the prescription about the killing may provide a clue to its meaning.[39] On the one hand, this act is distinct from the act of killing. On the other hand, it must be oriented specifically toward the act of killing itself rather than to the purpose of the killed animal for an עלה. It is also enacted before the killing of animals for other types of sacrifices. We must distinguish between the connection of firmly pressing the hand down and killing on the one hand and the connection of killing and its respective type of sacrifice on the other hand. The type of sacrifice is determined by the procedure with the already killed animal, not by its killing. Since the act of pressing down the hand is related to various types of sacrifices rather than to a specific type, it can only be related to that act in the sacrificial procedures that stands at the beginning of each procedure and is the same for them all. The position of this act immediately before the killing is, therefore, more than just natural or self-explanatory. Its meaning is specifically related to the act of killing.

It seems that pressing the hand down firmly is a distinct act by which the animal is officially surrendered to its subsequent sacrificial death. Since the animal's death happens for a particular sacrificial purpose and its killing is a ritual rather than a profane killing, this act commits it to its

---

[37] See B. JANOWSKI (1985: 240); R. RENDTORFF (1985: 34–48).

[38] So R. RENDTORFF (1985: 36–38). His interpretation that לכפר עליו in v. 4b(β) – interpreting v. 4b(α) – may refer to a certain, "nicht auf den Bereich der kultischen Sühne begrenztes Verständnis von *kpr*" (38) may remain problematic. It is more important that the phrase is generally recognized as a secondary redactional addition to ונרצה לו, which may as such infer into the notion of favor the notion of atonement originally not connected with v. 4b(α). V. 4b(α) refers to סמך in v. 4a, an act that has nothing to do with sin and atonement. The secondary addition לכפר עליו would thus have created a semantic tension in the extant text between the concepts of סמך ("pressing the hand down firmly") and רצון ("favor") on the one hand, and of atonement on the other hand. But it can scarcely have the weight to have reconceptualized the original concept to the extent that its original main notion was lost. As for לכפר עליו itself, the suffix to the preposition על points to "him" as the substantive subject of כפר, not to his "sin."

[39] Some exegetical statements come close. With regard to the dedication of the Levites, WRIGHT/MILGROM say that "Die Israeliten signalisieren durch ihre Handauflegung, daß die Leviten *ihre* Gabe (anstelle der Erstgeborenen) an JHWH sind"; a Hittite officer "legt im Ashella-Pest-Ritual seine Hände auf die Opferböcke und betet, die für die Plagen verantwortliche Gottheit möge die Gabe akzeptieren.... Da nichts auf eine Übertragung von Sünde hinweist, geht es auch hier um einen Dokumentationsritus" (886–7). R. RENDTORFF says the sacrificial animal is *übereignet* ("transpropriated") (1985: 29).

sacrificial killing itself, and not to the purpose of the particular type of sacrifice, whatever that purpose may be for the benefit of Yahweh, the offerer, or the priest. The act of pressing down the hand is the enactment of the offerer's decision to surrender the animal to death. This decision is, with perfect consistency, subsequently executed. It is an act of dedication to sacrificial death, *ein Akt der Übergabe an den Opfertod.*[40]

The main notion of the act of pressing the hand down concerns, therefore, the subjection of the animal to its impending fate of death, literally symbolized by the pressing down firmly of the offerer's hand. It is "his hand," יד׳, because it is his sacrifice which he gives. This subjection is not a magical but a legal act. It symbolizes the legality of his killing of the animal.[41] And it focuses on what happens through the offerer to the animal, not on the substitution for the offerer by the animal or on the flow of substance from the offerer to the animal.

At this point, the difference surfaces between two kinds of conceptuality: the meaning of pressing down the hand as such and the meaning of the text's prescription of procedure. Neither is made explicit, but each is

---

[40] This definition attempts to avoid one-sided alternatives: *Übereignung,* "transpropriation," implies the transfer of the animal, dead or alive, in a business transaction from one *owner* to another. But the sphere of death is not the animal's new owner. In the rite of the animal's passage, the sphere of death functions merely as the route for the animal's passage to its new owner, Yahweh. *Übergabe,* "surrender," to its death means instead that the animal is surrendered to this passageway. "Dedication" alone may refer to a new owner or a particular purpose of the sacrificial animal as well as to its fate of death. *Dokumentationsritus* is ambivalent because the offerer's right to his property, his *Besitzrecht,* could also be documented, apart from the fact that "documentation" can also refer to a written document. The expression "sacrificial death" is necessary, however, in order to avoid the connotation of profane slaughter, which is another reason why pressing the hand down firmly cannot be considered as a subsidiary act to the killing itself. For more specific differentiations between the notions of transpropriation and transfer, cf. 88−90 below.

The animal is the "victim" (Levine: 7). This word must be qualified. The animal's dedication of subjection to the fate of death is obviously not the result of a death sentence for its guilt. If anything, it is an innocent victim. The connotation of the victim's innocence is not impossible in view of the criteria for its selection, given in v. 3aβ, the reasons for which are, however, neither given nor operative for the selection. Nevertheless, this connotation, too, cannot be considered as the reason for its victimization. The animal is victimized neither for its guilt nor for its innocence, but because it is the offerer's gift to death for its passage to Yahweh in an עלה that has essentially nothing to do with anyone's guilt or innocence, or that at least exceeds the aspect of expiation for guilt possibly implied by v. 4bβ. Accordingly, the offerer's act of pressing his hand down firmly should in the proposed interpretation be assumed to mean a legally legitimate dedication or subjection to death rather than the result of a judically arrived at sentence of death.

[41] So also B. LEVINE: "the laying on of hands may not have been a cultic rite originally but, rather, a juridic or legal procedure" (6), which, I would add, it still is in our procedure.

exegetically important. The meaning of the act, just as much as the meaning of the entire עלה, is encapsulated in what happens to and with the animal itself, the עלה – קרבן. The meaning of the text's prescription of procedure, which focuses on what the participants must do, must then, if it is supposed to be proper procedure, intend to secure the implementation of the meaning of the sacrifice through its respective specific acts and their coherence in the total procedure. This means that the procedure is prescribed for the proper fulfillment of the sacrifice, and not for its own sake as an instruction for the mere mechanisms of the performance. The procedure, including its actants, is subject to the presupposed meaning of the nature of the sacrifice itself, in our case specifically, the fate and purpose of the עלה-animal.

At least one major connotation to the proposed meaning of pressing down the hand firmly must be noted, however: by imposing the decision of death on the animal, its owner surrenders at the same time his property. He officially gives it away as his living property, and the sacrificial purpose of this give-away for an עלה means specifically that he will no longer claim a share, even in the consumption or distribution of its dead portions, because it belongs to Yahweh totally. In this specific type of offering, we may speak of the this act as surrender to the animal's death for the sake of its *transpropriation (Übereignung)* to Yahweh, from one owner to another. In any case, the proposed understanding of the main notion of pressing the hand down and of its major connotation make it understandable why this act, too, after the ones referred to in v. 3aβ–bα, is considered or accepted in the offerer's favor. For his selection of the correct animal, his bringing it to the sanctuary and his enactment of its dedication to death, he is acknowledged appreciatively.

§11 רצון – Favor

What is the relationship between text and concept in the statements about רצון, vv. 3bβ–4b(α)? The text says that the offerer is the recipient of רצון. What he does not say but presupposes is that someone grants רצון. The expression of the text obviously focuses on the aspect concerning the offerer. At the same time, this focus cannot be isolated from the conceptual basis which involves a grantor as well as a recipient in the רצון-event, and not only a recipient or a grantor. We may assume, on intertextual grounds, that רצון is granted by Yahweh.[42] Indeed, Yahweh is explicitly understood as the one "before" whom the initial actions happen and who is the recipient of the עלה. However, the expression לפני יהוה in v. 3bβ says neither that he brings his gift "to Yahweh" nor that he receives favor "from Yahweh." Nor does he kill the animal "for Yahweh," v. 5a. The interpretive expressions in vv. 3bβ and 4b(α) point not only to the favor granted for each act referred to before these two phrases. They may also presuppose the inclusion of Yahweh in the conceptuality of the procedure in the sense that Yahweh's favor for the fulfillment of the procedural conditions thus far is made known to the offerer – just as the text makes this judgment known to the reader – through the mediation by the priest who would then be assumed to be involved at this stage of the procedure, before he begins to interact with the offerer from v. 5b on.

---

[42] See G. GERLEMAN (810), who refers to God's favor for the entire sacrifice when saying that "Die Wirkung eines dargebrachten Opfers hängt davon ab, ob es Gott gefällt oder nicht." This statement is acceptable with regard to texts in which the deity's favor is clearly granted to sacrifices. It must not obscure the fact, however, that רצון variously refers to specific aspects or acts in sacrificial procedures. RENDTORFF has correctly pointed out that it refers to the condition of the animal or to the sacrificial execution (35). We may add that in our text it also refers to the act of pressing the hand down firmly. The different positions of the expression in its context is one indicator for prompting such differentiations.

Excursus: The discussion about רצון

The current state of the discussion about רצון in our text remains complicated by the connection of רצון with the issue of imputation *(An-rechnung)* and of declaratory formula. The problem deserves a new, more extensive treatment. For the time being, the following should be noted.

The extant text does not use the lexeme חשב (see K. Seybold; B. Janowski: 217; R. Rendtorff: 36). It mentions no spoken declaration (see B. Janowski: 217; R. Rendtorff: 36). It says that favor is granted to the offerer by virtue of his own actions, and not that it is granted by virtue of a priestly declaration (see B. Janowski: 217). The text only states the fact of favor for the offerer, that it happens to him. It is also clear that the text focuses on the recipient rather than on the grantor or the mediator for the grantor, and that it points to the reason for the favor granted, namely, the offerer's bringing of the correct animal and his surrender of it to its sacrificial death – if the latter interpretation is sustainable.

From these textual data conceptual conclusions are sometimes derived which are not stringent. When B. Janowski says that "der göttliche רצון wird ... allein durch die rite vollzogene Darbringung zuteil ... *ohne* das Aussprechen einer priesterlichen Deklarations-formel" (217, his emphasis), he says more than the text permits. The fact that רצון is not granted *by virtue* (my emphasis) of a priestly declaration does not prove that it must have happened *without* a mediated declaration. It only means that רצון is not constituted by a declaration, whether it was spoken or not. Our – speechless – text allows no conclusion about either the absence or the presence of a spoken declaration. And should it be presupposed as being made, it would only have communicated Yahweh's valid judgment through the priest, but not constituted its validity.

When R. Rendtorff, following Janowski, abandons the connotation of imputation, *Anrechnung,* for רצון on the ground that our text refers neither to the verb חשב nor to a spoken declaratory formula, he also draws a conclusion that surrenders more than is necessary and allowable. Whether or not רצון connotes imputation depends neither on the presence or absence of the lexeme חשב, nor on a spoken declaration, nor on the fact that it approves of an offerer's act. As is true generally, this connotation may be conceptually implied without being explicitly named. The absence of the lexeme חשב does not prove the absence of the connotation in רצון of *Anrechnung*. Whether or not רצון connotes *Anrechnung* depends, therefore, on whether it is conceptually related to imputation in the sense that it refers to the substantively positive mental judgment with which a person credits another person. This meaning of רצון seems to be very much the notion of רצון in our text as it refers to both a fact expressed by the abstract noun, v. 3bβ, and an event expressed by the verb in v. 4b(α). For the time being, we should at least say that the discusssion about imputation, *Anrechnung*, cannot be considered as closed, even for our text. Indeed, the conceptual correlation of both notions, favor and imputation, seems to be closer than their separateness, if they are separate at all and for all their mutual distinctiveness. For this connectedness, see W. Schottroff, *"ḥšb,"* 643: "Charakteristisch ... ist die Parallele von ḥšb und ḥpṣ bzw. rṣh" (however, to what extent רנה should be considered in opposition to בזה "despise" [Schottroff: 643] is an open question since בזה refers to a substantively negative judgment whereas בזה refers to the formal mental judgment of either the approval or the disapproval of an action [Schottroff: 646]).

חשב designates a *Denkakt*, cf. G. von Rad (130); "eine einschätzende Bewertung" (W. Schottroff: 643); a mentally evaluative judgment. It means, among other things, to credit or debit a person for or with something (Schottroff: 644). It denotes a formal activity of the mind as such, and not the substantive outcome of a decision arrived at through it, and regardless whether that activity is verbalized or not. The same is true for רצון. The imputation of רצון may, but does not have to be spoken. It could be signaled by a silent gesture or by a non-verbal act or behaviour. In neither case is רצון constituted by the mode through which it is conveyed. The absence in our text of a reference especially to a spoken declaration, a *Sprech*akt, is, therefore, irrelevant for the question about a possible correlation of "favor" and "imputation," whether our text presupposes such a declaration or not.

However, the stated fact that רצון is attributed to the offerer presupposes that he is somehow informed about such imputation at this juncture of the procedure if the procedure is to continue – so according to this text. Somebody (who but the priest[s]?) has to inform him, and his resulting knowledge is the presupposition for the continuation of his actions. The act of information appears to be an important procedural element. Why does the text state only the fact of imputed רצון but not prescribe its procedural conveyance if it is concerned with proper, i.e., *rite* (Latin), procedure? Why are vv. 3bβ and 4b(α) formulated interpre-

tively rather than procedurally? Once such a prescriptive text projects
future procedure, it has an existence of its own, and these questions
cannot be answered with reference to assumed accidentalnesses of redactional operations. It prescribes a procedure for which the inevitable
act of the communication of favorable imputation is not prescribed
despite its importance for the continuation of the procedure. The answer
to the question may be found in a specific focus of the prescription, or in
what is meant specifically by proper or *rite* procedure, in an understanding by the prescription of proper procedure. Under this question, the
interpretive statements focus on what happens to the offerer himself
with respect to what he is doing rather than on what happens to his עלה
animal. The conceptual aspect of what constitutes *rite* performance
seems to focus on what happens to the עלה through the procedure, rather
than on the mechanisms of the procedure itself, let alone on the benefit
for the offerer.

Connected with רצון in our text is also the aspect of its validity or
legality. This aspect depends on the grantor of רצון, and not on its
priestly mediator or communicator, nor on the subjectivity of the offerer's insight. But it cannot be considered irrelevant because it constitutes
the basis without which the entire sacrifice would be invalid, already
disqualified at its early juncture. The statements about רצון in the text
must be considered as of binding quality. They are cult-legal statements.

Whether or not these statements themselves represent declaratory
language depends on how the word "declaratory" is defined. Just as the
Denkakt חשב was automatically linked with an oral *Sprechakt* (G. von
Rad: 130–133), so has the history of form critical research, due to its
prevalent interest in oral forms and settings and due to findings of
evidently oral formulations in biblical texts, perceived a text's declaratory statement *a priori* as an oral declaration. The definition of "declaration" was methodologically predetermined rather than based on a
scrutiny of its primary and secondary notions which would have opened
a wider field of biblical evidence. A declaration is certainly a linguistic
event. It is an official, formalized statement which authoritatively determines the nature of a certain issue. It can always be or become oral. But
its publication may also be originally written to be either orally pro-
claimed through the public reading of its text or simply silently read.
Indeed, the neutral and indirect formulations of many declaratory formulae identified in Old Testament research do not unequivocally reveal
the style of oral language, to say the least. The formulae in Lev 7:18b;

17:4; 13:8; Ezek 18:9bα cited by G. von Rad (131–133) are in their form not self-evidently oral, and are quite similar to those in Lev 1:3bβ–4b(α). Their corresponding expression in an oral setting may very well have required a transformation. And even if their extant form was also used orally, its origin may have been in writing. Therefore, if orality is to be the criterion for the identification of declaratory formulae, all formulae identified as such must be checked again as to whether or not they meet clear criteria for orality. Otherwise, declaratory statements will have to be defined by their own inherent characteristics. In this case, the statements in Lev 1:3bβ, 4b(α) may very well be considered as declaratory in the sense that the text itself declares to its reader that the favorable judgment imputed to the offerer is valid, authoritative, however this judgment is communicated to the offerer himself.[43]

---

[43] For the subject on declaratory language, see R. R. HUTTON.

§ 12 Lev 1:5−9

The prescriptions in vv. 5−9 thus far support the direction of the inquiry of the first three prescriptions in vv. 3 aβ, 3 bα, and 4 a. Based on the verb clauses, ten more prescriptions of distinguishable actions are listed *seriatim* in vv. 5 a, 5 bα, 5 bβ-γ, 6 a, 6 b, 7 a, 7 b, 8, 9 bα, for a total series of thirteen prescriptions in the apodosis of the subordinate case law vv. 3−9. There is a relative reason for discussing vv. 5−9 specifically, because they are united by the aspect of the dead animal. What constitutes the conceptual unity of this series?

It has been correctly implied that the sequence of the prescriptions listed does not reflect the sequence of the procedural acts envisioned by the list.[44] The difference between these two orders of sequence means, however, that at least from this point on in the text we must distinguish between the exegesis of the order of the text and our hypothetical reconstruction of the order of the procedure itself. It certainly is clear that from here on one cannot speak about the order of the text and of the procedure indiscriminately.

Despite occasional observations, this methodological distinction is by and large neither in principle nor in its effect on the exegesis of the text clearly worked out in the pertinent literature. R. Rendtorff's comments are symptomatic. E.g., he speaks about the sequence of the "acts" rather than of the "prescriptions," or that in v. 7 "wird der Ablauf der Opferhandlung unterbrochen," while in v. 8 "die Darstellung wieder zum Ablauf der Opferhandlung zurückkehrt" (1985: 55, 57, etc.). Of course, this sort of analysis of Rendtorff's, or any exegete's, diction should be taken for an unreasonable nit-picking on an otherwise clear meaning of what he/she says, if more were not at stake. Apart from the fact that the questions resulting from a consistent methodological distinction between the text's and the procedure's order could be worked out more

---

[44] K. ELLIGER speaks of the simultaneous "Hand-in-Hand-Arbeiten vom Opferherrn und Priester" (34−35). With regard to v. 9 a, R. RENDTORFF says that this "Vorgang" appears "verspätet" (1985: 59).

clearly,[45] there is a special reason for an actual recognition of that distinction. Rendtorff's exegetical diction is apparently based on his perception of the congruity of the text's *Ritual-Vorschrift* proper, "der eigentlichen Handlung," with the structure of the actual performance of the ritual. Should *rite* performance be required, the text itself would have to be a *rite* prescription especially as regards the "eigentliche Handlung."

The assumption of such a congruity presupposes, however, a qualitative differentiation between proper sacrificial and auxiliary or subsidiary actions in both the text and the hypothesized performance. In order to avoid a circular argument, one would have to identify the proper sacrificial structure of the text and of the performance independently of one another, and then conclude whether they are congruous or not. That is difficult to achieve. For the structure of the performed sacrifice proper one would have to have empirical evidence from observation. And even that would have to be explained in order to show how the distinction between proper sacrificial and auxiliary acts becomes perceptible in the performance of all acts together. And for the structure of the prescribed sacrifice proper one would have to show that the text itself clearly distinguishes between proper sacrificial and auxiliary actions. Evidence for the former distinction is virtually impossible. Evidence for the latter is at best subject to alternative interpretations because of the extent of the apodosis in the case law (just as in the analogous text), the coordination of the clauses, the presence of more perfect clauses than allowed for in the identification of the ritual proper, and a variety of aspects operative in the text, the signals for which seem to be more discernible than the signals for the distinction of proper sacrificial and auxiliary actions.

We must focus on the order of the text alone and, as a matter of principle, on its own system. According to v. 5a the animal is to be slaughtered by the offerer "before Yahweh." This prescription includes three aspects: 1) the actualization, the execution, of the offerer's surrender of his animal to its death, 2) the beginning of the entire process with the killed animal, 3) a distinctly intermediate act between v. 4 and vv. 6−9bα. The slaughter is certainly sacrificial, as the qualifier "before Yahweh" indicates. However, since animals are killed for a variety of sacrifices, the slaughter in this case begins the עלה process proper, too, but it does not yet identify the sacrifice as an עלה. The same is true for the

---

[45] On the basic reasons for this need, cf. what has been said above in § 6.

sprinkling of blood which is also prescribed for the שלמים זבח and, with variations, for the חטאת.[46] Only the prescriptions in vv. 6−9 identify the sacrifice as an עלה.[47]

Conceptually, then, the prescription for the עלה proceeds on the order of a pyramid turned upside down: it moves from the perception of the עלה as a component of קרבן in v. 3, which includes more than animal sacrifices, to its perception as a component of animal sacrifices in vv. 4−5, which is not yet עלה-specific, to the perception of the עלה-specific procedure in vv. 6−9. The עלה prescription is conceptually imbedded in the total sacrificial system, out of which its peculiar characteristics progressively emerge. We should assume that this conceptual presupposition is operative in the formation of the text.[48]

The individual acts of the procedure are scarcely "exactly described."[49] What controls the language of the individual prescriptions? Descriptive language would have to say, among other things, how, and not only that the acts are done. That is at best the case in vv. 4a and 5bβ. But how and where does the layman slaughter the animal, a bull or steer, v. 5a? Can he do it alone? If not, why are non-priestly helpers, e.g. Levites, not mentioned? How do the priests catch the blood, v. 5bα? How does the layman skin and dissect the animal, vv. 6a + b? These acts demand expertise in butchering, which is all the more important if the skin belongs to the priests and if the parts are not to be chopped to bits and are to be kept clean from accidental bowel spillage. No beginner can do that. How do the priests put fire on the altar − presuming that it must be done each time anew − and how do they stack the wood-pieces (עצים) up upon the initial fire to create a large fire required for such a large secrifice (v. 7a + b)? How do they arrange, set in order (ערך), the parts of the bull on the pyro-pyramid (v. 8)? Where is the water for washing the entrails and legs, and how does the layman (he alone?) protect the washed parts from contact with dirt if the animal is slaughtered lying on the ground (v. 9a)?[50]

---

[46] See R. RENDTORFF (1985: 53, and 97ff., 217).

[47] R. RENDTORFF (1985: 54).

[48] The systematization of the animal's species and the sacrificial genres referred to by K. ELLIGER (32) is indicated not only by the terminology. It can also be discerned in the presupposed conceptual coherence which is operative in the formation of the text.

[49] So R. RENDTORFF: "Die einzelnen Akte des Opfervorgangs werden genau beschrieben" (1985: 18).

[50] So R. RENDTORFF with good arguments (1985: 50). Of course, his − and others' − discussion of this point belongs no more to the text's "exact description" than all other

All these activities are consciously presupposed to be known. None is described at all, let alone exactly. Instead, the text's explicit prescriptions are obviously the result of a conceptualized, discriminating perspective about the constitutive acts in view of which all those related to them are adjudged to be subsidiary. The text represents not an exact description but a conceptually interpreted prescription of the constitutive activities.

---

questions about its exactness, or, it is just as much a discussion of the text's inexplicit presuppositions as it is the discussion of all other questions of that nature.

§ 13 Specific aspects

1. Clusters of actions

The thirteen actions prescribed in vv. 3aβ−9bα are individually distinguishable. Not each of them, however, is set apart from all others on the same conceptual level. The five actions in vv. 4a, 5a, 8, 9a, 9b are set apart from each other individually. The remaining eight actions are set apart from those five in four clusters of two each, vv. 3aβ + bα, 5bα + β, 6a + b, 7a + b. Each of these four clusters is conceptually united in contradistinction to each of the five individually characteristic actions. V. 3aβ + bα are united both by the aspect of the prestage before the actions at the sanctuary and their parallelistic formation; v. 5bα + β are united by the aspect of the blood-rite, v. 6a + b by the aspect of the dissection of the animal, and v. 7a + b by the aspect of the arrangement of the fire. This conceptual level assumes nine distinguishable stages of the total עלה procedure. Just as the inexplicit subsidiary activities are consciously presupposed for the explicitly prescribed individual acts, so are the thirteen individually distinguishable acts in the text conceptually presupposed to constitute the nine stages of the procedure.

2. The role of the actants

The role of the actants reveals more than a simple series of successive steps. Vv. 3−5a obviously envision the acts of the lay person in successive order. They are to be followed by two priestly actions in one stage, v. 5bα + β, but in successive order. The same cannot be said about the actions prescribed from v. 6 on. Is it necessary for the offerer to delay the animal's dissection until the priest has finished the blood-rite? After the killing of the animal and the priest's simultaneous catching of the blood he can start the dissection immediately, even while the priest carries and sprinkles the blood at the altar. The actions prescribed in v. 6a + b may begin simultaneously with those prescribed in v. 5bα + β. The presupposed simultaneous work becomes even clearer from v. 7 on. The starting of the fire (ashes from a previous fire have presumably been removed) with whatever is necessary to do this takes time, as does the subsequent arrangement of the wood pieces on the already kindled small fire. Especially, the development of the fire to a full conflagration, which is necessary before the considerable sacrificial pieces can be put upon it, takes some time. It takes about as much time, if not more, as it takes to dissect the animal.[51] Thus, whereas the actions prescribed in v. 8 must follow those prescribed in v. 6, those of v. 7 are understood as being well-synchronized with the offerer's work, and possibly as having begun at the outset of the entire procedure.

R. Rendtorff says with respect to v. 7: "Dabei wird zugleich der Ablauf der Opferhandlung unterbrochen, die den eigentlichen Opferakt, das Verbrennen des Opfertiers, vorbereitet" (1985: 55). This statement (already referred to in § 12), with respect to the tension between text and procedure, is also problematic because the procedure itself is said to be "interrupted." This means either that procedurally the processing of the animal is temporarily suspended – nothing happens with the animal while the priest is preoccupied with the fire (v. 7) – or that the sacrificial acts proper are interrupted by the priest's preoccupation with subsidiary, not specifically sacrificial, activities while the movement of the sacrificial acts proper involving the skinning and dissecting and placing of the animal upon the fire remains uninterrupted. It is not quite clear to which of these alternatives Rendtorff refers. He seems for either case to assume the exegetical distinction of proper sacrificial and subsidiary acts presupposed by the text but not explicit in it. The validity of this distinction depends on the criteria for a broadly based theory of sacrifice, in Rendtorff's case: his theory of the *Ritual*. If "interruption" refers to the temporary suspension of the procedural movement, it rests on the exegetical reconstruction of an equally unexplicated actual process for which we have no empirical evidence and which is at least very doubtful.

There is indeed little reason for the assumption of a temporary suspension of the "Ablauf der Opferhandlung." The actions of both actants are perceived to happen independently, so that neither actant must inactively spend time waiting for the other. And if we were to say that it is the

---

[51] See M. Noth's valid reference to the need for "ein mächtiges Feuer" (1962: 14).

text that suggests such an interruption, we would be on equally weak grounds. The text expresses only the connectedness and flow of the actions. Any interpretation of their interruption rests on what the text might presuppose conceptually but not on what it says. K. Elliger, also reconstructing the envisioned sequence of the actions, says that the priest starts the fire "nach dem Blutritus" (35). His statement means at least that the priest starts the fire while the offerer skins and dissects the animal, v. 5. But even that is not necessarily so. The blood may very well be sprinkled, tossed low and round about at the altar's walls[52] after the fire has been set and is blazing upon it. Finally, the washing in v. 9a should be considered as coinciding with the priest's actions prescribed in v. 8. Only the priest's action stated in v. 9bα is presupposed to take place after all else is completed.

3. *The distribution of the work*

K. Elliger has emphasized two conceptual aspects: "die rechte Verteilung der anfallenden Arbeiten" and "das Hand-in-Hand-Arbeiten" of offerer and priest.[53] Indeed, the text is explicitly concerned with the acts and the working *(den Arbeiten* and *dem Arbeiten)* of the two participating parties in the procedure. An interpretation based on the verbs alone, defining the procedure in terms only of its acts, without including the text's references to the different actants, leads to a wrong perception of an important aspect in the conceptuality of the text. Nevertheless, Elliger's exegesis is still problematic. It infers that the text presupposes the participants' interaction or collaboration in their work. This inference is not self-evident. It is at least in need of qualification.

The two aspects of distribution *(Verteilung)* and collaboration *(Hand-in-Hand-Arbeiten)* are neither identical nor equally significant. The aspect of distribution of work is clearly indicated by the separate cultic identities of the two parties, and by their separate actions at separate places. The aspect of their collaboration may be exegetically postulated, but necessary qualifications relativize it as such and particularly in comparison with the aspect of the distribution of their work. Collabora-

---

[52] K. ELLIGER (35); so M. NOTH (1962: 13); R. RENDTORFF (1985: 52).

[53] K. ELLIGER (34). Note the twofold meaning of ELLIGER's usage of the German word "Arbeiten" in the sense of *die* Arbeiten, "the works, actions," and *das* Arbeiten, "the *(worker's)* work*ing,* do*ing.*"

tion is only "visible" (*sichtbar,* Elliger: 34) in vv. 5a + bα, in 8 and 9a + bα. The actions referred to in vv. 4a, 5bβ, 6, 7, as well as those in vv. 3aβ + bα, have nothing to do with collaboration. Collaboration is not the dominant presupposition for the whole text, neither for a unit vv. 3−9 nor for a unit vv. 4−9. Nor does collaboration reflect a two-way procedure between altar and place of slaughter. The collaborative actions take place at the place of slaughter. They involve the priest's, not the offerer's, coming from and returning to the altar, once to catch the blood and repeatedly to pick up the animal's parts. Strictly speaking, it is the priest who takes over the work with the animal from those acts of the offerer that represent the limit of what he himself may do with it. The priest makes the decisive implementation of the offerer's עלה possible by transferring it to the altar − whence the fire transmits it to Yahweh. [54] To whatever extent the aspect of the distribution of work is important for the text, it is certainly more encompassing and especially more important than the aspect of collaboration or interaction.

The text supports these qualifications. It says only what the respective parties must do with the animal, but not what they do together or to each other such as passing the animal one to the other or taking it one from the other. Their work is controlled by what must be done to the animal, especially in order to process it through the עלה procedure. This aspect conceptually unites their mostly separate and partly connected work. Much more than by the aspect of the distribution of work, however important that is, and still more than by the aspect of collaboration, the text is apparently governed by the aspect of the participants' actions for the sake of processing the עלה itself. This aspect constitutes the criterion for the integrity of the עלה procedure. This conclusion about the main generative conceptuality is supported by the *waw*-consecutives which, irrespective of all other aspects, point to the cohesiveness of the conceptual coherence in the text's surface and to the forward moving nature of the text itself which reflects the forward moving nature of the envisioned procedure. [55] The forward moving prescriptiveness, which does not correspond to the reconstructable sequence of the actions, reinforces the

---

[54] The number of actions prescribed in vv. 4−9 amounts to five for the offerer and six for the priests (but if v. 3 is included, seven for the offerer); whereas of the nine identified stages of the total procedure, five fall into the offerer's (vv. 3aβ + bα, 4a, 5a, 6a + b, 9a) and four into the priest's responsibility (vv. 5bα + β, 7a +b, 8, 9bα). These indicators point to the distribution of the work.

[55] For the perf. consecutive forms, see R. RENDTORFF (1985: 59).

impression of the text's own conceptual priority of the actions as a forward moving procedure over the other aspects.

This interpretation also differs from Elliger's emphasis on the correctness or properness of the distribution of work, "die *rechte* Verteilung" (34, emphasis mine). It is difficult to rationalize why this aspect should dominate the *Niederschrift,* even if it should be the text's instructional intention. If anything, this sort of distribution is basic for the sacrificial texts and belongs *a priori* to everyone's presupposed knowledge of the sacrificial practice. As much as, if not more than, anything else presupposed but not said, the prescriptions for the sake of this instruction were very unnecessary. They would amount to carrying "water into the Rhine" – unless one assumes an original text or an original tradition which knew only of one actant, the offerer, and no priest, a text or tradition against which the prescriptions of our texts would introduce a drastic reconceptualization through which the sacrificial institution should fall under the decisive hierocratic control.[56] Evidence for the assumption of such a reconceptualization is lacking. The question, however, as to what extent the text is interested in the proper execution of the sacrificial procedure, "im richtigen Vollzug des Opfers" (R. Rendtorff, 1985: 62), involves more than the aspect of the proper distribution of its work or the proper performance of the individual acts. In as much as "properness" is involved for the prescribed law, it is the properness of the total procedure rather than, or at least more than, the properness of its individual acts or of the participants' collaboration or distribution of work.

4. The quality of the acts

The text presupposes that the prescribed individual acts are of different importance. They have different sacrificial qualities. Already the dif-

---

[56] In his 1954 dissertation, R. RENDTORFF had argued for a place of the priest, הכהן, only in v. 9bα of the original text of the Ritual (1954: 11). Already K. KOCH saw a larger role for the priest in the original Ritual (1959: 47). But even then, the priest was for RENDTORFF not absent from the ritual entirely. In the meantime, he has adjusted his earlier position to the one expressed by K. ELLIGER, who said: "die Abgrenzung der Funktionen zwischen Priestern und Laien ist vielmehr schon integrierender Bestandteil der Ursprungsform der Gattung" (31). RENDTORFF confirms – though without abandoning his claim to the genre Ritual – by saying: "Der Versuch, aus dem Subjektwechsel literarkritische Folgerungen zu ziehen ... hat sich nicht bewährt. Insbesondere lassen sich daraus keine unmittelbaren kultgeschichtlichen Schlüsse ableiten" (1958: 51).

ference between the explicit prescriptions and their presumed, inexplicit subsidiary activities indicates this qualifying discernment. But qualifying distinctions are also operative in the text directly. The offerer's selection and bringing of the animal to the sanctuary are required under cultic qualifications, and most probably require approval. The same is true for his following acts of pressing the hand down firmly and of killing of the animal, whereas skinning and dissecting — and perhaps also the washing?[57] — of it are scarcely of equal, let alone higher, sacrificial significance.

Similar distinctions apply to the acts of the priest. His bringing, and especially his sprinkling, of the blood at the altar, and his causing "the whole," הכל (v. 9 bα) to be consumed by fire on the altar are the focus of the text, whereas his production of the fire itself and even his arrangement of the animal's parts upon it are again sacrificially less relevant.[58] For either participating party, the text seems to presuppose a qualitative differentiation between sacrificial acts proper and supporting, practical acts necessary for the procedure.[59] Also, the priest's activities — for the

---

[57] The washing of the entrails and legs may be more significant. The entrails, which must also be burned, must be washed of their — unclean — feces whether they were accidentally sliced open at the dissection or not. The legs must be washed because they, or at least their lower limbs, are probably not skinned. They not only become dirty as the carcass lies on the ground; they may be even unclean as the animal is still alive. By contrast, the animal's trunk seems to be in no need of washing because it is dissected upon the skin laid out underneath it after the skinning. The trunk remains, therefore, protected from contact with the ground or floor. The washing may qualify as a side-action, *Nebenhandlung* (R. RENDTORFF, 1985: 59), if all such washing is a ritual side-action, a problematic qualification in view of the need to keep anything unclean away from the altar and from Yahweh. Just as with other ritual washing, it is certainly more than a matter of practicality or aesthetics. Its qualitative degradation on the ground of the text's stylistic change (RENDTORFF, 1985: 59) is not persuasive. In fact, its possibly secondary redactional insertion could have happened precisely because of its ritual importance rather than because of its minor significance.

[58] This judgment is defensible in view of the comparison of the starting of the fire and the arrangement of the wood with the sacrifice proper of the animal. It does not mean, however, that the activities concerning the fire and wood are irrelevant. The word ערך itself, together with its nominal form מערכה, is "part of the technical vocabulary of the cult" (Levine: 7).

[59] Though more in passing than systematically, and with differing assessments, the commentators' interpretations point to the qualifying differences in the text. E.g., M. NOTH says that in v. 2b (better: v. 2aβ) "beginnt der eigentliche Ritualtext" (1962: 12). In this text, he distinguishes between "der eigentlichen Opferdarbringung," apparently according to vv. 8–9, the preparation for it according to vv. 6–7 and, so by inference, the prestages to the preparation (whether according to vv. 2b–5 or only vv. 4–5 is not clear [13]). R. RENDTORFF, also assuming a text, says that "das eigentliche Ritual" begins in v. 4

sake of the offerer and not withstanding the fact that the עלה is initiated by the offerer[60] — appear to be more significant than the offerer's own.

Excursus: The sacrificial quality of the blood-rite

The question of the sacrificial quality of the blood-rite should probably be distinguished from the much-discussed question of the meaning of the blood itself. Neither is explained in the text. However, while the latter question implies an ontologically based answer such as "the life of all flesh is its blood," Lev 17:14; Deut 12:23 — a question to which the answer is scarcely presupposed or required to be known for the performance of the blood rite, the answer to it, even if known, does not answer the former question why the animal's blood must be tossed at the four sidewalls of the altar. The answer to this question *is* presupposed to be known by the priest, if for no other reason than that the blood must neither be spilled at the place of slaughter nor be burnt with the animal on the altar. R. Rendtorff, who finds no connection between the blood-rite and the sacrifice proper, explains the blood-rite with reference to the repeated prohibition against eating blood: conceivably, it is to withhold the blood from human consumption (1985: 53). But prevention from human consumption is true for the entire עלה animal. In this instance one would have to say that the blood must be spent together with the total עלה animal because nothing of the עלה may be eaten, not only not the blood. If this is the only concern, the blood might as well be spilled at the place of slaughter in order to comply with the prohibition against eating it. But it must instead be tossed at the altar! The aspect of the blood-rite is governed by where the blood goes, not from whom it is withheld.

K. Elliger comes closer when saying that the altar is "der Ort der besonderen Gegenwart der Gottheit" (35). But this answer, too, does not explain why the blood is to be tossed against the altar rather than

---

(1958: 32), which means that vv. 2aβ–3 do not belong to the Ritual-text proper. The Ritual describes an *Ablauf der Opferhandlung* which consists of seven individual ritual acts (1985: 32, 48, 51, 53 ["kultischer Gesamtvorgang"], 54, 55, 57, 59, etc.). Within this series of seven ritual acts, however, there are *Nebenhandlungen* ("side-acts") (1985: 55, 59) and, consequently, also the ritual acts proper. Each commentator points to a different set of qualifying criteria. The interpretation of the text's qualifying system is open.

[60] R. Rendtorff: "Der Opfernde bildet den Ausgangspunkt für die Darlegung" (1985: 21).

burned upon it with the animal. M. Noth may come closest in explaining
both: the blood is tossed against the altar as the place which belongs to
the deity. And because, so we continue, the blood *does belong* to God –
a priori – it cannot be part of the offerer's sacrificial gift burnt with his
gift upon the altar. It must instead in a separate act be surrendered to
Yahweh at his altar and – quite consistently with Yahweh's *a priori*
ownership of it – before the offerer's own sacrifice is spent by the priest
upon the altar as a gift to Yahweh in the sacrifice proper! That means,
however, confirming Rendtorff's disclaimer of a connection of blood-
rite and sacrifice proper, that the blood-rite, though belonging to the
total עלה procedure, is not an element of the offerer's sacrificial gift. It is
not specifically sacrificial. This result should affect the discussion of the
extent of the sacrifice-ritual. It is at least obvious that a distinction must
be made between the meaning of the words "ritual" and "sacrifice."
Nevertheless, one cannot for these reasons say that the blood-rite had a
cultically subordinate quality. Its quality rests on its exceptionality as
Yahweh's *a priori* property, and not on its comparison with the quality of
the sacrificial gift.

5. The participants' knowledge of the value system

The text and the involved persons envisioned by it cannot be unaware
of the qualitative differences of all these actions. The dimension of their
awareness of these qualities should in our interpretation not be excluded
from their knowledge of and focus on their acts themselves. The acts are
qualified, and qualified with differentiations. Their differentiated
understanding rests on the knowledge of a value system rather than on
the knowledge of the performative technicalities. And although these
qualifications, and the awareness of them, belong to the conceptual
matrix of the text, they rightly belong to its exegesis because their signals
are discernible on its surface.

Nevertheless, the qualities of the individual actions do not yet reveal
the qualifiers for the totality of the prescribed עלה procedure. Its totality
is more than its individual acts or their sum total. The עלה procedure has
its own distinct qualifiers which are different from those by which the
individual acts are qualified. The total prescription is indicated by the
waw's. By connecting the sentences they signal the *cohesion* (Utzschneider: 15–16) of thirteen individual prescriptions and the pro-

cedure's envisioned acts, and also the unity of the procedural movement. Yet neither the otherwise identifiable qualities and kinds of
coordination of the prescriptions or those factors that qualify the procedure as a whole are so signaled. Those factors are also not found on the
higher, conceptual level of the identifiable nine stages of the prescribed
procedure.

Within each of the four stages vv. $3a\beta + b\alpha, 5b\alpha + \beta, 6a + b, 7a + b$,
two successive acts are coordinated. But even more the stages themselves are coordinated. None of them is isolated in the sense that it would
be relevant without all others, let alone replace them. The kinds of their
coordination are variable, and even their qualities differ. The vari-
abilities and differences of the stages indicate that the constant or
constitutive aspects for the prescription must be sought in those qualifiers that are germane to the coordination of the stages themselves.

Excursus: The position of v. 9a in the text

Why is the prescription for the washing given at its place in v. 9a of the
text? This question is by no means superfluous. The writers could have
placed this prescription for seemingly obvious reasons after v. 6a + b,
their prescription for the offerer's flaying and dissecting of the animal.
Does his washing of its entrails and legs not necessarily and directly
follow his dissection of it? Did the writers miss that aspect and insert the
prescription for his washing of the animal as a *"Nachtrag"* at its present
place, the only place left if it had to be mentioned before their concluding statement in v. 9b? Furthermore, the question would not be answered with reference to redaction-critical arguments, even if they are
based on legitimate observations.

1. K. Koch has in his most recent 1990 essay ("Rituale") addressed the
question of the position of v. 9a in brief but intensive fashion. His
interpretation is pregnant with complex implications, and deserves care-
ful analysis. He says (1990: 77−78) − so I understand the substance of
his argument − that v. 9a was positioned after vv. 4−8 (but inevitably
before v. 9b) because it refers to what Rendtorff calls a *Nebenhandlung*.
The prescription for this side or auxiliary action was added by the writer,
the *Schriftsteller,* at its extant place in the course of the transposition of
the "Ritual" from its originally oral form into a written text (its *Verschriftung*). This addition was necessary because of the writer's interest
in purity. Rather than being positioned between vv. 6 and 7, its seeming-

ly appropriate place, it was positioned after vv. 4—8 because it presupposes a circumstantial side-aspect and not the main aspect of the sequence of ten actions *(Folgehandlungen)* which controls the original "Ritual" expressed in perf. forms. The problem apparently centers around the role which the aspects of *Nebenhandlungen* ("side or auxiliary actions") and *Folgehandlungen* ("consecutive actions") are assumed to play in the position of v. 9 a in the text.

Koch's conclusions rest once again on the assumption that the perf. forms are, with Rendtorff, generically basic and indicative of, against Rendtorff, an originally *oral* "Ritual." My own findings, in addition to those of others, do not provide sufficient evidence for preferring these assumptions to alternative options. Also, the basis for the assumption of *Nebenhandlungen* in which Koch follows Rendtorff is more than problematic, especially in as much as it is supposedly indicated by the difference between perf. and imperf. forms. In fact, for this assumption Rendtorff distinguishes not only between ten perf. forms and one imperf. form, but also between seven ritual acts proper and three "nicht eigentlichen" sacrificial acts within the ten prescriptions in perf. form, which I take to mean *Nebenhandlungen.* Rendtorff does not, so it seems, equate in the final analysis the ten perf. forms with reference to ten sacrificial acts proper. His interpretation of *Nebenhandlungen* includes some in perf. form. It is, therefore, in addition to the criterion of the verb forms, based on the evaluation of qualitatively different ritual actions. The results from the employment of both criteria are in tension, if not in contradiction. For the specific discussion, see especially sections 7 and 13 of this study.

One may ask why washing in a ritual procedure should be considered as a *Nebenhandlung,* especially if it is necessary for the sake of purity (!), and why the prescription for it in imperf. form should indicate its lower ritual validity. Ritually, it seems to be more important than, or at least as equally important as the actions referred to in Lev 1:5 b, 7 a + b. In Exod 29:17 bα it is prescribed in perf. form. Does that form not qualify it as a ritual act proper, a *Haupthandlung?* Should we assume a degradation of ritual washing during the process of transition from the oral to the written stage of the claimed Ritual? For such an assumption, we would have to have separate substantive rather than grammatical evidence. It does not seem that the imperf. form in Lev 1:9 a can be taken as an unquestionable signal for a *Nebenhandlung,* quite apart from the fact that it can still be explained by the inverted syntactical structure of v. 9 a.

That also means that the argument of *Nebenhandlung* does not provide sufficient explanation for the position of v. 9a after vv. 4−8. Even accepting that argument, including the use of the imperf. form, the prescription could well have been placed after v. 6b.

Koch's other argument for the position of the prescription at v. 9a rather than after v. 6b is that the prescription was not positioned according to the aspect of consecutive, ritual acts *(Folgehandlungen)*. Of course, since the determination of *Neben-* and *Folgehandlungen* is at least to a great extent the result of the exegete's evaluative judgment rather than of the text's explicitness, the question arises (but will here be left open) as to whether the denial of the aspect of *Folgehandlung* for v. 9a is not more a *logical* consequence from the presumed equation: perf. form: *Folgehandlung* = imperf. form: *Nebenhandlung,* than it is the consequence of exegetical observations arrived at for each type of action independently of the other. At any rate, Koch attempts to support his own argument against the aspect of *Folgehandlung* in v. 9a − which is obvious but in my opinion based on different reasons − by a comparison with Exod 29:17. That passage shows, according to Koch, that the instruction for washing the entrails and legs is placed appropriately under the aspect of *Folgehandlung,* namely, between the instructions for dissecting the ram and for putting (them) "upon" its pieces and "upon" its head, and the instruction to "cause the whole ram to smoke" on the altar follows. Indeed, that text appears at first glance to be ordered according to the sequence of actions: the washing of the entrails and legs presupposes at least their separation from the animal's corpse and probably also the dissection of the animal, and most probably is delayed until the dissection is complete. And they may be put upon the pieces and the head and smoked on the altar only after they are washed.

Nevertheless, the assumed aspect of consecutive actions must be qualified. It does not necessarily mean that the entrails and legs are washed *before* the pieces and the head are put on the altar. Since they are put "upon" the pieces and "upon" the head, as the text says, the pieces and head must have been put on the altar earlier, and probably in successive order as they are successively dissected. Such an interaction between the successive dissection of pieces and head and their simultaneously successive transport to and upon the altar scarcely allows for the offerer's simultaneous washing of the entrails and legs. Their washing would have to wait until the dissected parts are dispensed with, at least until the successive handover of piece after piece to the priest for their immediate deposition on the altar fire is complete. The washing will come *after* those interactions of dissection and deposition on the altar which does not mean that the entrails and legs are not washed before they themselves are put on the altar.

The apparent aspect of the sequence of actions *(Folgehandlungen)* in this text is, therefore, generated but also controlled by the focus on the typology of actions signaled by the verbs alone, and on the sequential relationship of the kinds of actions, but not on a sequence of actions involving the different parts of the animal. If the latter were the case, the position of the instruction for washing the entrails and legs should be found in Exod 29 after, rather than before, v. 17bβ. And Koch's statement that the prescription to wash these parts stands "an der wirklich zutreffenden Stelle *im Ablauf der Begehung*" (1990: 78, emphasis mine) may amount to the opposite of what the text permits. Only one thing is certain: both dissecting and washing must be completed before all parts may be put on the altar.

The qualification of the aspect of sequential order implies the question of whether or not the criteria for this type of order are the same in each text. The answer to this question can only depend on the observations gained from each individual text. It cannot be *e silentio* presumed as a given pattern. In a comparison of Exod 29:15−18 with Lev 1:3−9, the position of Exod 29:17bα before v. 17bβ indeed indicates that the aspect underlying the position of the washing in Lev 1:9a cannot be the same as in the Exodus text. That does not mean, however, that the only option left for the position of Lev 1:9a, as an alternative to the aspect of *Folgehandlung,* is the aspect of *Nebenhandlung.* Had Exod 29:17 been controlled by the primary aspect of the simultaneous interaction between the ram's dissection and deposition on the altar, the aspect of the sequence of actions would be subordinate to this primary aspect and the instruction for the washing would perhaps have been positioned after v. 17bβ, in exact parallel to its position in Lev 1:9a. Such a position would by no means point to a *Nebenhandlung,* whether expressed in perf. or in imperf. form. Yet even as such a position may be *caused* by the primary aspect of simultaneous interaction, it does not *eo ipso* mean that by now this aspect represents the only possible reason for the position of the instruction or prescription.

More would have to be said about the comparison of the two texts. They are not only similar but also dissimilar for several reasons. Lev 1:3−9 cannot be said to follow the shape of Exod 29:15−18. Especially on the basis of Rendtorff's and Koch's grammatical criteria, assuming that the washing in Lev 1 is as important as it is in Exod 29, the prescription for the washing in Lev 1 should neither be expressed in the imperf. form, nor positioned in v. 9b, nor evaluated as a *Nebenhandlung*. Or conversely, in addition to the arguments gained from within Lev 1:3−9 against a *Nebenhandlung*, it is difficult to see why the washing in Lev 1 should be understood as such a side-action while the same cannot be assumed for the Exodus text. But if the imperf. form cannot be considered as the signal for a *Nebenhandlung*, the basic rationale for the explanation of the position of Lev 1:9a has disappeared. To be sure, the inverted form will have to, and may still be, interpreted, with Elliger and others, with reference to stylistic convention. But even this reference does not explain why v. 9a is positioned in its present place rather than (even in imperf. form) between vv. 6b and 7. Koch is correct when quoting Elliger's reference to inversion and saying: "Warum aber aus-gerechnet *Eingeweide und Wadenbeine* hervorgehoben werden, erklärt er" − Elliger − "nicht" (1990: 78n.11; emphasis mine). However, while Rendtorff and Koch attempt the required explanation, the evidence for their explanation is less than persuasive, and the position of v. 9a must (and I believe can) be explained otherwise.

Koch is nonetheless on the right track when pointing in his just-mentioned footnote to the entrails and legs. In Exod 29, the reason for the formation of the text is the sequence of the types of acts themselves rather than of the treated objects. In Lev 1, the reason for the position of v. 9a is neither the aspect of successive acts nor the distinction between ritual acts proper and auxiliary acts, but is instead the differentiation of the various parts of the animal to be treated with respect to their deposition on the altar. In this respect, Exod 29:17 already gives a clear signal. By instructing the animal's dissection into "its pieces" (לנתחיו) and the washing of "its entrails and legs," and then saying: "And you put (them, i.e., the entrails and legs) upon its pieces..." (על־נתחיו), the text explicitly distinguishes between the "pieces" other than the entrails and legs and the "entrails and legs" in addition to the pieces. The "entrails and legs" are not considered as part of the "pieces." This distinction is also true for Lev 1:9b + 8aα on the one hand, and for v. 9a on the other hand. The only difference is that, while this distinction is not the domi-nant aspect for the formation of Exod 29:17, it appears to be the reason for the position of v. 9a in Lev 1. What must be explained, then, is the reason for this distinction itself. We may not be able to explain what the writers intended to say. But we may be able to discern what the text means in what it says.

2. The prescription presupposes the text's perception of the anatomy of the animal and of the processing of its parts in the procedure. V. 9a refers to the animal's "inward part," קרבו, sing. (which, however, is a collective expression for the entrails specifically) and to its legs, כרעיו. The apposition in v. 8aβ, את־הראש ואת־הפרד, refers to the head and the fat, by which the fat means specifically the fat around the entrails, the kidneys, and the liver rather than all fat in the animal's body; cf. Exod 29:13, 22; Lev 3:3−4; 7:3−4; 8:16, 25; etc.

The pieces of the dissected animal mentioned by the text are, therefore: from its body, the head and the legs, and from the inside of its body, the particular portions of fat and the entrails. Where is the reference to the largest part of the body, the trunk or torso, the body itself exclusive of the head and the limbs, and the other components inside the body? The text does not mention these, yet can hardly be unaware of them. We must assume that they are originally, inclusive of head and fat but exclusive of entrails and legs, referred to in v. 8aβ, "the pieces," הנתחים. For whatever reason, the following redactional apposition has obscured the original meaning of v. 8aβ by actually limiting "the pieces" to head and fat only, thereby eliminating the torso and its parts from the meaning of הנתחים, "the pieces." Despite that redactionally created semantic tension, however, we must assume that reference to the torso is still presupposed in "the pieces." That means, however, that the text presupposes a process in which the parts of the torso, together with the head and the fat (mentioned separately through all parts of one stage) are said in v. 8a to be arranged on the fire prescribed in v. 7 and this process is assumed to be fully developed by the time the acts of v. 8a happen. It also means that v. 9a is not prescribed earlier in the text because the washing of the less important entrails and legs is associated with the prescription for the burning of "all," את־הכל, in v. 9bα, which takes place after the arrangement of the most important pieces on the altar. This understanding also suggests, literary critically, that the position of v. 9a is not in conflict with the semantic inclusion of the torso in "the pieces," v. 8aβ, and therefore not dependent on the later redactional addition of the apposition "the head and the fat" in v. 8aγ. Unless separate evidence exists for a literary layer secondary to the one indicated by the perf. form construction, there is no reason for assuming such a layer for v. 9a on the ground of its inverted imperf. construction. V. 9a belongs to the same layer to which vv. 4−8 belong.

Therefore, the position of v. 9 a in the text has nothing to do with the question of the simultaneous or successive order of the acts, i.e., whether the washing of the entrails and legs (only those!) takes place while or after the main pieces of the animal are put on the altar and burned. It is relevant for the position of v. 9 a that it is considered as the preparation for the final stage of the transfer of the last, and least important, parts of the rest of the animal to the altar so that now the whole can be consumed. That final stage is expressed in v. 9 bα, and v. 9 a expresses the preparation for the final stage and therefore belongs to it. It must be noted that v. 9 bα says not "he arranges," ערך, as v. 8 does, but "he causes to smoke," הקטיר, which presupposes the arrangement while expressing its effect. Similarly, "the whole" in v. 9 bα refers no longer separately to the pieces but collectively (including the final pieces) to the priest's completion of the already happening fiery consumption of the עלה. In sum, v. 9 a owes its position to the text's conceptual perception of the coherent movement of the total sacrificial procedure toward its goal.

§ 14 The unity of the text

1. Direct signals

The coordination of all stages is more than and different from the significance of each stage. It points to the aspect of the unity of the text. That unity is above all concerned with procedure. To whatever genre our text may specifically belong, it belongs first of all to the genre of procedural rather than substantive law. Intrinsic to this genre is its focus on procedure which implies, self-evidently, proper procedure. The concern for proper procedure reflects administrative settings in which and for which guidelines are established for the objectified implementation of individual cases. And since procedures differ typically because of typically different administrative settings and their needs, the coordination of the stages in any procedure depends on the typicality of a particular setting, in our case, the system of the sacrificial cult.[61] This system consists of several sacrificial types, each of which requires its own procedure. Our text focuses on such a type. It is עלה specific. It prescribes the specific procedure for the עלה of a steer/bull in which the thirteen individual steps and their nine coordinated stages are coordinated under the unifying aspect which identifies the whole prescribed procedure as בקר-עלה specific. It is, therefore, concerned not so much with proper as with specific procedure. One should assume anyway that the aspect of properness is automatically connoted in any prescription of procedure.

---

[61] Traditionally, the critical exegetical discussion including the form critical discussion of the macro-genre case law has been preoccupied with the legal traditions outside the cultic settings, without sufficient attention to the fact that this genre was also applied by the cultic institutions. This one-sided socio-linguistic perspective appears to be another heritage from the original assumption, according to which the case law tradition belonged to the civil and the "apodictic law" to the cultic domain. In the meantime, it has become clear that a typical legal form does not belong to one setting only. The consequences of this insight have yet to affect fully our understanding of the connection of case law and cult in particular, and our understanding of the complex relationship between genres and the historical sociology of ancient Israel and the Ancient Near East in general.

What, then, is procedure-specific in the prescription for the עלה of an exemplar from בקר? The answer to this question must be sought in those aspects that determine and control this total procedure including its coordinated steps and stages, so that this kind of עלה may fulfill its objective. The prescription of the procedure, or this procedural law, is generated by the substantive criteria that are necessary for this fulfillment. When speaking about criteria we refer neither to substantive law nor do we lose sight of the aspect of procedure. On the contrary, the prescribed procedure is itself the result of substantive conceptual aspects that lie underneath the text and guide its formation.

What are these aspects? In addressing this question we must of course be aware that no specific aspect concerning the בקר exemplar can be dissociated from its central purpose as an עלה. Any such aspect is subordinate to the aspects pertaining to that purpose in the same עלה text. While the procedure for the treatment of an exemplar of עוף, vv. 14−17, is obviously different from the procedures for exemplars referred to in vv. 3−9 and 10−13, and while there are also intratextual differences between vv. 3−9 and 10−13 themselves which may point to some procedural differences as well as to the literary and conceptual dependence of vv. 10−13 on the paradigmatic text vv. 3−9, it is clear that the contingent conceptualization of each subtype depends on the basic aspects of its purpose as an עלה. Our focus on these aspects in vv. 3−9 does not mean that all procedures are presumed to be exactly identical. It only means attention to the בקר procedure as עלה specific.

The text, including the introduction, gives direct signals. The עלה, a subtype of קרבן, is a gift for Yahweh (v. 2aβ). The animal for the עלה, an ox, is selected and brought to the sanctuary, and there acknowledged to the favor of the offerer before Yahweh (v. 3aβ + b). It is symbolically surrendered to its fate of death, for which the offerer is also acknowledged favorably (v. 4a + b), and subsequently killed before Yahweh (v. 5a). The blood which *a priori* belongs to Yahweh and is not a part of the offerer's sacrificial gift must, therefore, be tossed at the altar before the gift for Yahweh can be processed (v. 5bα + β). Above all, (and without which no act or stage would be sufficient) the flayed, dissected, and (where necessary) washed ox is, through its fiery consumption on the prepared and blazing pyro-pyramid, offered totally and alone to Yahweh (vv. 6−9bα) as an עלה gift of pleasing/soothing odor (v. 9bβ). These direct signals already point to more than the technicalities of the prescribed meaning of the procedure, or to more

than a meaningful procedure: they point to a total sacrificial gift for
Yahweh.

Excursus: עלה אשה ריח־ניחוח ליהוה

V. 9bβ contains three specific problems. For one of them, the translation of אִשֶּׁה, we can follow R. Rendtorff's critical discussion. The word
means "das, was von den Opfern Jahweh gegeben wird und darum ihm
gehört," or "<Gabe> im eigentlichen Sinne des Wortes" (1985: 65, 66).
The two other problems are: does ניחוח mean *Wohlgefallen* ("pleasedness"), or *Beschwichtigung, Beruhigung* ("appeasement," "soothing"),
and does ריח־ניחוח refer to the nature of the (offerer's) gift, אִשֶּׁה, or to
the significance of the gift for Yahweh? Each question affects aspects of
the other.

First, what does the noun ניחוח mean? The history of its interpretation is divided between *Wohlgefallen* and *Beschwichtigung*. The difference is significant, because it presupposes two different kinds of relationship between Yahweh and the offerer, or more precisely, two kinds
of relationship of Yahweh to the offerer, normal or disturbed. In a
normal relationship, ניחוח can only mean pleasedness or pleasing, but
not appeasement. In a disturbed relationship it can mean either pleasedness or appeasement, whereby pleasedness would be a function of
appeasement since appeasement can scarcely be unpleasant or unpleas-
ing. It is clear that either pleasedness or appeasement has something to
do with Yahweh because it is apparently the kind of Yahweh's relationship to the offerer to which his עלה responds. But it is not clear which of
these two kinds of relationship the word ניחוח presupposes. The word
itself is, therefore, open to either of the two meanings.

Nor it is clear whether the meaning of the word refers to the offerer
despite the fact that it has something to do with Yahweh, or whether its
point of reference is something else still. It may refer to the party which
pleases/appeases or intends to do so, or to the party which is pleased or
appeased or is about to become so. Or it may refer to the medium which
has, for whichever party, either for effect or purpose, a pleasing or
appeasing odor. Again, the word is open to any of these possibilities, and
its particular meaning can only be discerned from its specific context.

ניחוח can syntagmatically be determined, as it belongs specifically to
ריח. It qualifies ריח, "odor," in one of two possible ways: either as an

odor of pleasantness alone, a pleasant odor *(ein angenehmer Geruch)*,"
whereby the atmospheric aspect of a good-smelling odor is apparently
the presupposition for its pleasing function; or as an odor of appeasement, which includes its pleasantness as a precondition. And since the
formula ריח־ניחוח is directed by the preceding noun אִשֶּׁה in construct
form, it qualifies that "gift" as having an odor of pleasantness or of
pleasing appeasement, or perhaps of appeasing pleasantness. It seems to
be clear that ריח־ניחוח does not refer to the offerer, neither to what he in
effect achieves nor to what he intends to achieve. The phrase refers to
the offerer's gift, his עלה, the word which opens v. 9bβ. In the end, the
decisive event takes place in what happens between the offerer's gift and
Yahweh, not between the offerer himself and Yahweh.

Still unresolved is whether the gift's odor of pleasantness or appeasement refers to its purpose or to its effect on Yahweh. The phrase
אשה ריח־ניחוח would in the first case refer to the purpose of the gift only,
but in the second case to the positive result of that purpose. The preposi-
tional phrase ליהוה at the end of v. 9bβ does not solve the open
questions. It may refer to the entire preceding phrase אשה ריח־ניחוח or
to ריח־ניחוח alone. In neither case does it clarify whether the "gift of
pleasing odor" or the "pleasing odor" is only pleasing to Yahweh or also
appeasing to him, and whether either of these two readings refers to the
purpose or to the positive effect of that purpose on Yahweh.

The following contextual and intertextual observations may be helpful.

a) The phrase under discussion explains the phrase עלה הוא (cf.
1:13,17) which in turn classifies the total prescribed procedure. So R.
Rendtorff (1985: 62) following B. Janowski (222). This procedure is a
particular kind of offerer's "gift for Yahweh," vv. 2aβ, 3aα. If analogous, v. 9bβ, too, would speak about the particular kind of "gift for
Yahweh." In both instances, it is seen from the perspective of the
offerer's gift rather than from the perspective of its effect on or reception
by Yahweh. Should v. 9bβ be seen from Yahweh's perspective as well or
instead, it would, either in part or entirely, stand in tension with the
perspective of the prescribed procedure and the expression "gift for
Yahweh" in v. 2aβ. Such a conceptual tension in the same context is not
impossible, but in view of the possible conceptual coherence in this
context it should not be assumed unless there is stringent evidence for it.

b) The preferred impression of conceptual coherence just mentioned
is supported intertextually by passages such as Gen 8:21; Lev 26:3; Ezek

6:13; 16:19; 20:8; and also 20:41. They all have in common the fact that ריח־ניחוח refers to the kind of odor of the human presentation which, of course, reaches Yahweh so that he smells it. In no case, however, does this kind (ניחוח!) of odor as such predetermine the effect on Yahweh, namely, whether he will be pleased or appeased by it. Nor does it determine Yahweh's reaction, namely, whether he will accept or reject it. Yahweh may be pleased or appeased or not, and accept or reject ריח־ניחוח. ריח־ניחוח predetermines none of these possibilities.

c) For the phrase אשה ריח־ניחוח ליהוה, the distinction between the notion of its nature as a human gift and the notion of its effect on Yahweh is, therefore, fundamental. The phrase does not refer to the effect on or the kind of reception by Yahweh, be it pleasing or appeasing. This result speaks against K. Elliger's specific formulation which says that the phrase means "das Sichversichern," assuring oneself of support through a positive effect on Yahweh (36) and especially against F. Stolz who says that the odor of appeasement "bringt so das Verhältnis zwischen Mensch und Gott in Ordnung," again referring to effect (*"nūᵃḥ*," 1976: 46). Except perhaps for one word, K. Koch is correct when concluding, on the basis of religio-historical considerations, that "Für P und Ez bedeutet rêaḥ-nîḥôaḥ demnach der <wohltuende Geruch,> der beim festlichen Opfer entsteht und das rechte Klima für den segnenden Umgang Gottes mit der Kultgemeinde schafft. Deshalb erwartet Ez 20:41 davon <Wohlgefallen>" (445). As long as ריח־ניחוח "creates" only "the climate" "für den segnenden Umgang Gottes...," it only establishes the purposive function of the odor of the gift as a presupposition for the deity's responding "segnenden Umgang." Yet this pleasing odor does not yet predetermine the divine blessing response in the sense that it establishes or creates that blessing, or that it restores a disturbed relationship. K. Elliger, while being on the incorrect track with his "sichversichern," is in the same sentence correct when speaking about "die Huldigung gegenüber einem Mächtigen, das *Werben* um sein Wohl*wollen*" (36, emphasis mine). (See also R. Rendtorff's [1985: 68] statement that the offerer's gift is presented "in der *Erwartung* und *Hoffnung*" to be accepted by Yahweh [emphases mine].)

d) By comparison, the aspect "wie das Opfer bei der Gottheit <ankommt>" (R. Rendtorff, 1985: 68) does not appear to be the distinctive point in the phrase ריח־ניחוח. Apart from the necessary distinction between the notions of the gift's arrival (a *Tatsphäre*-notion) at Yahweh, and the kind of reception by Yahweh, the phrase and all its parallels self-evidently presuppose that ריח־ניחוח does arrive at and is received by Yahweh as an either pleasant or − meant to be − appeasing odor. Yet this presupposition is not the focus of the phrase.

e) The following possibilities remain: the gift for Yahweh that has a pleasant odor is given with the *purpose* of either pleasing or appeasing Yahweh. That it functions under the one or the other of these *purposes* must once again be presupposed. The gift is *purposeful*. The notion of a presupposed purpose is an element intrinsic to the meaning of the gift. V. 9bβ refers to the odor of the gift as purposed for achieving either Yahweh's pleasure or appeasement. It focuses, then, coherently on the one aspect of the offerer's gift itself, and represents a "Doppelausdruck" (R. Rendtorff, 1985: 68), at best in the sense that it reflects both the nature of the gift and the gift's addressee from the one vantage point of the gift's purpose, but not in the sense of two vantage points, one from the deity and the other from the offerer.

f) If the aspect of purpose, or of hoped for rather than actual effect, is common to the different notions of pleasing and appeasement, this common denominator seems to relativize the difference between the two notions. Whether the pleasantly smelling gift is to please or to appease, it is given in the hope of, but without the definitive certainty of, being accepted. Surely, the sacrificial institution established and sanctioned by Yahweh is the ground for the legitimacy of such hope and expectation. It provides a degree of certainty. But it is the certainty of legitimate hope for, rather than the certainty of, the acceptance of the pleasantly smelling gift.

Of course, the gift of an עלה in the hope of being accepted by Yahweh has nothing to do with human self-redemption through the cultic act, as much as this act is subject to a specific procedure prescribed specifically. B. Janowski, following others, is correct when emphasizing atonement as *Heilsgeschehen* throughout his work and especially pointing out, following Schaeffler, that the cultic performance is based on the *Gründungshandlung der Gottheit* which (so I prefer to interpret) establishes the legitimacy of hoped for acceptance as Yahweh's own sacrificial gift through his establishment of the sacrificial system.

g) The element of hope or expectation associated with the gift is an anthropological correlative to the purpose of the gift itself. The text's awareness of hope despite the indefiniteness of the result has two implications, one about Yahweh and the other about the offerer's condition. On the one hand, it indicates that Yahweh is understood to remain the

Lord of his cult and its sacrifices. He is not replaced by the cult. Even in its most correct (should *rite* be decisive) or meticulous observance, the sacrifice remains subject to Yahweh's judgment, and the offerer's dependence on an עלה is no substitute for his dependence on Yahweh. One cannot say that the prophetic protest against a perceived autonomy of the cult is exclusively rooted in a specifically prophetic notion of Yahweh's sovereignty. This notion is shared by the priestly theology, and it may well be that the prophetic protest against its perversion is validated by the fact that it reflects the tradition of the priest's own theology rather than an alternative, anti-priestly, specifically prophetic theology alien to the priestly tradition.

On the other hand, the awareness that the עלה-gift is expected or hoped to be positively accepted may, despite the known indefiniteness of its result, shed some light on the question as to how important the relative difference still is between the gift's pleasing or appeasing function. If the major purpose of the gift is its acceptance. Yahweh may accept it either by being pleased or also by being appeased. The עלה is given for either possibility. Its main task is to fulfill, through its finally pleasing odor, the end result of the procedure: the condition that it may be accepted for either possibility. The openness for either possibility points back to an open question in the offerer's situation which may be the cause for presenting an עלה, and not another type of sacrifice, in the first place. It points to a situation of the offerer's uncertainty about Yahweh's relationship to him, to which his עלה responds so that Yahweh, depending on his own predisposition, may be either pleased or appeased.

h) This interpretation leads to consequences for the translation of the phrase. Critically important for the translation is the distinction between the different referential aspects in what the phrase says. In one syntagmatically possible point of reference the "odor of the gift" would express its resultative or effective function: it pleases or appeases, is in effect pleasing or appeasing Yahweh. The fact that it may please the offerers themselves is irrelevant. This point must be ruled out on the basis of the semantics in the text's conceptuality. It cannot even be considered as a presupposed connotation of the notion proper of the phrase.

In reference to the purposive function, the phrase would express the purpose of the "odor of the gift": to please or appease Yahweh, regardless of whether it either does or does not. This purposive function is indeed operative in the text, but only as a presupposed connotation of its

notion proper. The distinction between these two referential aspects
leads to the distinction between the phrase's own notion, its notion
proper, and its connotations of which — in our case — one is an operative
presupposition whereas the other, while syntagmatically possible, is not.
And since the difference between "to please" and "to appease" falls
under the purposive aspect, this point of reference, too, belongs to a
presupposed connotation rather than being expressive of the notion
proper of the phrase. Our analysis has concluded that the notion proper
of the phrase refers to the fact that the odor is pleasant *(angenehm)*. The
translation must render this notion. V. 9bβ should be translated: "a
burnt/whole offering, a pleasantly smelling gift, for Yahweh," or "... a
gift for Yahweh which has a pleasant odor"; in German, "ein Brandopfer, eine angenehm riechende Gabe, für Jahweh," or "... eine Gabe
für Jahweh von angenehmem Geruch." Since this translation results
from the discernment of several referential aspects, it certainly must be
accompanied by commentary. Once again, we are reminded of the
difference between translation and exegesis, but also of their interdependence.

i) The proposed interpretation and translation of v. 9bβ may help to
shed some light on the opposing exegetical positions concerning "pleasing" and "pleasant" *(erfreuend* and *angenehm)* and "appeasing" or
"soothing" *(beschwichtigend* or *beruhigend)*.

J. Milgrom comes close when saying that "the *'ōlâ* serves other functions, e.g., petition ... and thanksgiving.... The *'ōlâ,* then, is all encompassing; it answers to all emotional needs of the worshipper"
(1976: 769). (See also R. Rendtorff, 1976: 74−89.) It is indeed encompassing, and covers many possible needs for the worshipper to react to
Yahweh's predisposition, however that need may be felt emotionally.
Yet if it can, among other things, also serve as a thanksgiving for a
received blessing, e.g., for a just-received expiation, how should the
same act serve at the same time as an offering for needed expiation? It
seems that its "all encompassing" range involves not only expiation of "a
much broader scope of sins" than those involved in חטאת and אשם, which
"expiate for the limited sins of the pollution and desecration of sanc-
tums," but also functions in matters other than those falling under
expiation/atonement.

K. Elliger, after identifying ריח־ניחוח syntagmatically as an attribute
to אִשֶּׁה, says that "P denkt gewiß an die Beschwichtigung des göttlichen
Zornes über die Sünde," although he realizes that the phrase is missing

in the texts about the sin — and guilt — sacrifices. Thus, he admits that its meaning is "von Haus aus allgemeiner," referring to homage *(Huldigung),* wooing *(Werben)* for goodwill, for assuring oneself *(Sichversichern)* of support, all of which has nothing to do with sin, as the examples of Noah's good-smelling sacrifice shows (Gen 8:21). Nevertheless, so Elliger, the later P theology understood the phrase sharply as "<Beschwichtigungsgeruch> des göttlichen Zornes," which implies a knowledge of the irrationality of that anger (35−36).

B. Janowski (217n.176) follows Elliger's interpretation, although he points out very clearly that the phrase ריח־ניחוח is only very infrequently and secondarily connected with texts about the sin and guilt sacrifices. His comments imply that ריח־ניחוח at least originally could not have referred to appeasement for the sake of expiation/atonement.

According to Elliger's exegesis, the phrase ריח־ניחוח expresses nothing but the function of the odor: either it may be to please or appease (purposive), or it may in effect please or appease (resultative). Not considered at all is the possibility that this attributive phrase does not refer in its notion proper to any function of the odor at all but only to the aesthetic atmospheric quality of the gift of a pleasantly smelling odor. If this is true, the understanding of the gift's and its odor's function would have to be derived from the presupposed but not explicated purpose of the עלה itself, a purpose presupposed to be known and therefore in no need of explanation because this knowledge constitutes the criterion for the offerer's choice of an עלה in the first place.

Also, Elliger's interpretation of the semantic shift in the formula's tradition history is ambivalent: if the formula was originally *allgemein,* it must have encompassed a pleasing and an appeasing function. If it had been "sharply" reduced in P to an appeasing function, its meaning would have shifted from its encompassing function to this specific function only, and the עלה would have served nothing else but the expiation of sin, only now in the sense of all-encompassing sin, a sense analogous to Milgrom's interpretation. But the evidence for such a traditio-historical development is shaky. The priestly concept of עלה points to more than expiation of sin in its wider sense. And the assumption of this shift does not explain why the priests should have excluded a traditional function of the עלה such as a gift of thanksgiving for received blessing, which encompassed more than the response to sin even in its widest sense. (See R. Rendtorff, 1967: 74−89.) We must apparently account for a different development: that the originally wide range of occasions for an עלה,

which later lost its dominant role to the חטאת, retained this wide range nonetheless (Rendtorff, 1976: 88) and even expanded it by including such occasions that involved the offerer's uncertainty about Yahweh's predisposition toward him, occasions that did not specifically belong to the condition for sin or guilt offerings. In this respect, Elliger's statement about "the knowledge of the irrationality of the divine anger" (36) deserves consideration, if only with the modification that divine anger is perceived as a possibility rather than as an irrationality. But it must be repeated that the discussion about the traditio-historical aspect of the shift in function is concerned with the function of the עלה itself. It does not affect the thesis that the main notion of the phrase ריח־ניחוח refers to the gift's odor.

M. Noth says that the phrase "Feueropfer beruhigenden Duftes für Jahweh" is a "überaus massive Aussage über die intendierte Wirkung ... des Opfers." What is intended here is "die Beschwichtigung" of real or possible (!, not irrational) divine anger (1962: 14). Noth uses the words *beruhigend* and *Beschwichtigung* synonymously. In his exegesis the aspects of purpose and effect are related not in the sense of achieved but of intended effect, which is correct. Yet again, the phrase ריח־ניחוח is considered by Noth to refer to this intent directly or mainly, and its meaning is specifically narrowed to the contestable purpose of soothing or appeasement alone. The possibility that the phrase might express the nature rather than the intention of the gift's odor is again ignored. This despite the fact that his formulation of "beruhigenden Duftes" points to that possibility in the main notion of the phrase: that it refers to the *Duft* itself as intended to be *beruhigend*. Consequently neither the different referential possibilities nor the differentiation between the notion proper and the connotations in the formula come into clear focus, and the exegetical result remains unsubstantiated, ambiguous, and, in our case, improbable.

R. Rendtorff translates: "Ein Brandopfer (ist es), eine Gabe beruhigenden Duftes für Jahweh" (1985: 16). He explains "daß der Duft des Opfers <beruhigend> oder <befriedend> wirken *soll*" (68, emphasis mine). His exegesis makes clear what his translation leaves open, that ריח־ניחוח refers to the intended and not to the actual effect. It refers to the purpose of the gift. The other problem arises with what is intended, which is said by Rendtorff to be *beruhigend, befriedigend* ("calming," "pacifying"). This terminology points to a presupposed condition in which Yahweh is not calm or pacific, and which is the cause for and purpose of the gift. It belongs to the semantic range of (intended) appeasement of divine anger or irritation, whether clearly perceived or only suspected, rather than to the range of the pleasantness, or its intended pleasingness of the gift itself, or to a normal or normalized relationship. This understanding, however, suggests a purposive function of the gift's pleasant odor within the concept of expiation, of removing the causes for "real or possible divine anger" (Noth, 1962: 14), even at the expense of a more inclusive function of the עלה. And it does not clarify the tension between the expiatory connotations of the gift's pleasant odor and Rendtorff's otherwise distanced stance from an assumable expiatory function of the עלה. Also, the possibility that the phrase may in its notion proper refer to the nature of the gift, literally, its *Natur,* rather than to any connoted function is, once again, not considered in its own right.

B. Levine translates: "an offering by fire" (!, for אִשֶּׁה) "of pleasing odor to the LORD" (7), and explains with "a pleasant aroma," and "a pleasing odor" (8). The two explanations do not mean the same thing. The first refers to the atmosphere of the aroma, adjectively called "pleasant," whereas the second, adverbially, refers to its pleasing function. He qualifies this functional explanation saying that we have "reason to suppose that such" (a pleasing odor) was *"intended"* (8, my emphasis). Yet he also says in his interpretation of v. 9b that "the sacrifice" (properly considered) "counts in his favour" (6), and that "the favorable acceptance of the *'olah* signaled God's willingness to be approached and served as a kind of ransom, or redemption, from divine wrath" (7). If I conclude correctly, Levine's interpretation means that the pleasant odor of the עלה, intended to be pleasing, counts in the offerer's favor in the sense that the עלה is accepted by God as a sign of his willingness to be approached and served for ransom. In this sense, the odor is both pleasant and intended to please, whereby its pleasing function would presuppose, and therefore be a connotation of, its pleasantness. The intent to please is without basis if the odor is not pleasant in the first place. Indeed, it is, as Levine remarks, following Maimonides, "the use of incense as a means of removing the stench of the burning sacrifices" (8) is for what purpose if not to turn that stench into a pleasant odor so that it can serve the intent to be pleasing. Hence, the primary notion or notion proper of ריח־ניחוח is the one of a "pleasant odor."

A tension remains, however, in Levine's statements that the odor is *intended* to please and that the עלה, for which the odor of the transmuted animal stands, is *accepted* by God. The first statement refers to the sacrifice's intention, but the second to its positive effect. Yet it is not self-evident that the formula refers to both at the same time, not even by the phrase ליהוה. Levine's statement about acceptance suggests perhaps the qualification on his part that the עלה is only accepted as a sign of God's willingness to be *approached and served,* rather than as a sign for his willingness or decision *to accept the effect* of the approach and service of ransom itself. The latter is perhaps what Levine means, anyway. If not, the formula would still be said to refer to God's acceptance of the intent, if only, so to say, as a matter of still further consideration on God's part and, hence, not to the final acceptance of the עלה. Such an assumption would be difficult to verify. Should acceptance of the approach's effect be meant, i.e., acceptance of the עלה, the formula would again refer to both the intent and the acceptance, and that remains an open question.

j) The ambiguity in exegetical work concerning the semantic difference between "pleasing" *(wohltuend)* and "calming/appeasing" *(be-ruhigend/beschwichtigend)* is probably not coincidental. As long as one assumes that ניחח is an adverbial (pleas*ing*/appeas*ing* = *wohltu*end/ *beschwichtig*end) rather than an adjectival (pleas*ant* = *angenehm*) attri-bute of ריח, one is left with the alternative between pleasing or appeasing for the interpretation of the notion proper of the phrase. Once its main notion is understood to denote the pleas*ant*ness of the *odor,* the adver-bial function of ניחח appears as a presupposed but inexplicit connota-tion − in terms of purpose − of its main notion, which may be under-stood in terms of pleasing as well as appeasing. This understanding blends with what is known about the variety of the functions of the עלה which concern sin in a wider sense and also other occasions not requiring expiation or atonement. Thus, while explicitly referring to the nature of the gift's odor, the phrase presupposes that the purpose of this pleasant odor is, depending on the particular purpose of an עלה-gift, to be either pleasing or appeasing. This conclusion affects the understanding of "cultic expiation/atonement" *(kultische Sühne).* The עלה is in each case a cultic act, and the pleasant odor is the final result of its procedure. However, not each עלה and, hence, not each pleasant odor is necessarily concerned with cultic expiation or cultic appeasement. We must there-fore distinguish between the cultic act in each עלה and not only the different situations in life that prompt sacrificially different genres of cultic gifts and sacrifices but also specifically different occasions for and functions of the עלה itself. The עלה, including its final pleasant odor, reflects and responds to the variety of such life situations as it embraces several possible functions.

k) The proposed understanding of the phrase ריח־ניחוח collides with לכפר עליו in 1:4bβ if that phrase refers only to cultic atonement or expiation. However, R. Rendtorff has concluded that v. 4bβ is not confined to the realm of cultic atonement (1985: 38). According to his interpretation, the phrases in vv. 4bβ and 9bβ, therefore, do not conflict. But it is not clear why in view of his interpretation of v. 4bβ he nonetheless translates the phrase by "ihm Sühne zu schaffen" (1985: 15). Whatever כפר in v. 4bβ means, it takes place in a cultic procedure. If in such a procedure it refers to something in addition to atonement, why is the text translated by "Sühne schaffen"?

B. Levine says that the sense of expiation "is not suitable here because as a type of sacrifice the 'olah was not occasioned by any offense that would have placed the offender in need of expiation" (6–7). By contrast, what is needed is "redemption" for "protection from God's wrath" because "proximity to God was inherently dangerous for both the worshipper and the priests, even if there had been no particular offense to anger Him. The favorable acceptance of the 'olah signaled God's willingness to be approached and served as a kind of ransom, or redemption, from divine wrath." Because of a different context, part of this statement already quoted before is quoted again. Apart from the alternative between "expiation" and "redemption," Levine's interpretation of לכפר, v. 4bβ, presupposes that its redemptive function is accomplished by "the favorable acceptance of the 'olah," the sacrifice in its entirety.

This presupposition is problematic because it is an open question whether or not the whole עלה is understood in its final effect, resultatively, to be accepted "favorably." It is also problematic because its position in v. 4bβ relates the phrase to the reception of favor (v. 4bα) for the act of pressing the hand down firmly (v. 4a). It is, therefore, at least doubtful if the phrase can be taken as referring to "the favorable acceptance of the 'olah."

But especially problematic is Levine's overall argument which says that the עלה as such, by being favorably accepted, grants redemption from God's wrath concerning the proximity to God which is inherently dangerous for both the worshipper and the priest. If redemption is necessary because of the proximity to God, because of the worshipper's and the priest's dangerous position "before Yahweh," v. 3bβ, "a defined sacred area" (Levine: 6), why does the phrase לכפר עליו only speak about redemption "for him" and not also for the priest who, even more than the offerer, is exposed in this sacrificial procedure to the proximity to God because of his work at the altar? And if this dangerous proximity to God is the reason for necessary redemption through favorable accept-ance of the entire עלה, why should the offerer not simply stay at home, away from the danger, rather than come to the dangerous sacred area, there draw the wrath of God, and be for that reason forced to offer an עלה for favorable acceptance?

But our case law presupposes that he decides to bring an עלה to the sanctuary for whatever life situation has caused that decision, perhaps an experience of God's wrath in that situation − as Elliger has pointed out. And should לכפר עליו refer to the result of the entire עלה, it would mean "ransom, or redemption, from divine wrath" for that life situation rather than for his proximity to God. He brings an עלה to the sanctuary because of − possibly but not exclusively − God's already-experienced wrath, but not because of God's wrath experienced as the result of his coming to the sanctuary. The עלה is not offered for redemption from wrath necessi-tated by proximity to God. If anything, it is offered, at least in this case, to overcome God's distance from the offerer and to bring the offerer into God's proximity. If לכפר עליו refers to the entire עלה, it can only refer to the offerer's situation before he decided to offer an עלה. Whether or not the phrase refers to the meaning of redemption only, or the meaning in this text of expiation only, or to both, is under discussion, including the question of its reference to v. 4a only rather than to the entire עלה.

According to B. Janowski, following Elliger and others, v. 4bβ does refer to atonement (216−218). He qualifies this in the sense that the phrase refers to the atoning function of the entire עלה rather than to the act of pressing the hand down firmly only (216), and that the *"homo peccator"* symbolically identifies with the sacrificial animal through the firm placement of the hand (220−221). On the "Identifizierung des Opfernden mit seinem Opfer," see also K. Elliger (34). In these qualifi-cations, it is not clear whether the phrase v. 4bβ is seen in light of the assumed atoning function of the עלה, or whether the atoning function of the עלה is seen in light of the interpretation of v. 4bβ in terms of atonement. Without v. 4bβ, the עלה may be, but does not have to be, atoning. This also means that the firm pressing down of the hand in the עלה procedure does not have to symbolize the identification of a *peccator* with the sacrificial animal, quite apart from the different conclusion about the meaning of this act arrived at in this study (cf. above, § 10). Likewise, v. 4bβ ‾may, but need not, in this text qualify the entire עלה as atonement for sin, especially if one considers its unusual position so early in the text. This position makes it possible to interpret לכפר עליו as referring, together with ונרצה לו in v. 4bα, to the result of the firm pressing down of the hand alone rather than to the entire עלה.

N. Kiuchi assumes "that כפר על means 'make atonement for'," and also "that the atonement (לכפר עליו)" in Lev 1:4b "is the purpose of the acceptance of the entire sacrifice" (117). The present study qualifies both statements.

H. C. Brichto says about Lev 1:4 (not 1:14!): "An Israelite offering an 'ōlā is to place his hand on the animals head ... to win him (divine) favor by providing composition in his behalf (lekapper 'ālāw). It is the 'ōlā offering in its totality which so serves" (31). Brichto arrives at this conclusion in the context of other passages discussed on pp. 31–34, according to which the "kipper-act" is fulfilled by the entirety of the sacrifice. His contextual argument cannot be ignored. It is also registered by R. Rendtorff (1985: 37–38), who points out, however, that in all instances concerning the חטאת, the kipper-act is consistently stated at the end of the text, whereas "Lev 1:4" – an עלה text – "ist die einzige Stelle, an der der Ausdruck כפר mit der Handauflegung verbunden ist" (37). It is not self-evident in this text that the total statement of v. 4 stands for the totality of the עלה, especially when one allows that כפר does not signify atonement or expiation exclusively.

Indeed, Brichto's discussion points to a basically different meaning. Seeing kipper as derived from kōper he says: "The biblical context of kōper is most closely approximated by the term 'composition' in its legal sense, the settling of differences. An imbalance between two parties (individuals, families, clans or larger social groupings) results from a damage or deprivation inflicted upon one by the other. Equilibrium is restored by a process which consists of a transfer of something of value (a person, an animal, or a commutation of such in the form of commodity or currency) from the injuring party to the injured. The acceptance of this value-item by the latter, itself termed 'the composition' (as is the process itself also), serves to 'compose' or settle the difference" (27–28). Hence, Brichto translates לכפר עליו in Lev 1:4 with "by providing composition in his behalf" (31). Summarizing, he says that the verb kipper "is never clearly or satisfactorily attested in the sense of expiate or atone" (34), and especially that "every offense against Deity requires a *kōper* (as, indeed, does many an unsalubrious condition involving no offense).... To offer/make composition, to accept composition — is the basic force of *kipper*" (35).

Brichto's interpretation of "composition" by way of a *transfer* of value coincides with what in § 10 of this study is called the *transpropriation (Übereignung)* of property — certainly for restoring the equilibrium (Brichto, Rigby) between the parties. The only difference is that the transfer happens, according to Brichto, through the עלה in its entirety, whereas the present study distinguishes between two aspects in this transfer which are encapsulated in two complementary acts: the act of the animal's legal transpropriation through the dedication to its sacrificial death, symbolized by the firm pressing down of the hand, and the subsequent implementation of this legal transpropriation through the animal's physical transfer to Yahweh. This distinction does not mean that the "composition" and transfer happen by what is said in Lev 1:4 alone, instead of what is said in vv. 5–9. It only means that the acts prescribed in vv. 4 and 5–9 represent two aspects of the same entire עלה-gift: the legal and the physical gift of the animal. Their successive performance means that the legal side of the gift, symbolized by the firm pressing down of the hand, enacts the legitimacy of the following surrender of the animal to its death whereas its physical side, the killing and processing of the animal, implements the offerer's enacted decision to transpropriate it. The distinction between these aspects in the two acts seems to account for the position of the interpretive statements v. 4bα + β in the context better than the assumption that לכפר עליו refers to the entire עלה regardless of its syntactical and semantic connection with the act of pressing the hand down firmly.

However, this distinction within the same concept of transpropriation-transfer may help to explain why the phrase לכפר עליו, meaning "by providing composition in his behalf" (Brichto), could be placed either at the end of a text about a specific procedure or, as in Lev 1:4bβ, in connection with the statement specifically about the pressing of the hand down firmly. In either position, the phrase refers to the settling of a difference, a disturbed equilibrium, through transpropriation and transfer. And while its normal place at the end of the pertinent pericopes indicates conventionality, its exceptional place in our text points to an emphasis on the aspect of the legality or licitness of the offerer's decision, which is favorably accepted for the purpose of providing composition for him, rather than to an emphasis on the final effect of the total עלה-gift on Yahweh's acceptance.

To be sure, what has been said indicates that the aspect of atonement implied in the formulaic and semantic nature of the phrase לכפר עליו in Lev 1:4bβ cannot be entirely ignored. [62] It seems that the often-observed secondary, redactional edition of the phrase, especially at its extant position, has in this case injected into the text a genuine bivalency and ambivalence. Under the influence of this ambivalence, the act of pressing the hand down alone or the entire עלה text may be read as a prescription of an עלה for the purpose of atonement for sin in a wider sense, and v. 9bβ would then have to be read as connoting intended appeasement only, rather than as intended pleasing. At the same time, however, the traditional functions of the עלה, which included more than the concern for atonement, can scarcely have been totally eliminated or "energisch unter den Gesichtspunkt der Sühnebeschaffung gerückt," as the result of a religio-historical reconceptualization in which the meaning of the entire sacrificial institution was seen "nicht mehr in der Freude vor Jahweh wie im Deuteronomium, sondern nur noch in der Entsündigung und dadurch der Erringung des göttlichen Wohlgefallens" (K. Elliger: 32 – 33).

For the assumption of such a radical reconceptualization, the comparison between Deuteronomy and P, in the sense of joy, *"Freude"* versus legalistically understood liberation from sin, *"Entsündigung,"* offers no basis in the first place. Deuteronomy's appeals to joy are based on the parenetic and therefore inevitably psychological language and intentionality of Deuteronomy. The priestly legal corpus is composed in "legislative" language. It is not parenetic. If one wants to compare the psychological aspect of joy with the legal aspect of law, *"Gesetz,"* one will have to ask how the two corpora, each within itself, use both legal and psychological language. It will quickly become clear, then, that Deuteronomy proclaims law as well as it exhorts and admonishes to keep the law with joy, indeed, that its proclamation of the law is reinforced rather than replaced by its parenesis. And it will also become clear that P's primary interest in formulating laws, especially laws about the pro-

---

[62] So also H. C. Brichto: "In the cult system the necessity to effect composition through an offering ... is what accounts for the metonymic extension of *kipper* to equal *ṭiher* or *ḥiṭṭē'*. Since composition is a prerequisite for forgiveness, the metonymic extension of *kipper* in quite another direction can be discerned in its meanings remove, wipe away, erase, annul and, even upon occasion, to expiate" (35–36).

cedures for the liberation from sin, does not mean that their religion was without joy, *"freudlos,"* and that they could not have appealed to the psychological effect of joy in the experience of the liberation from sin had they wanted to do so. On occasion, as in Exod 35:4f., 22–29; 36: 1–7, their texts point to this dimension, and with quite an unmistakable parenetic intention for their readers. But this psychological factor also plays a role in the text's presupposed knowledge of the human conditions which prompt sacrifices, especially voluntary decisions for sacrifices intended either to please or to appease Yahweh. The generally accepted interpretation − the hope and expectation that these sacrifices may be accepted − points to the psychological implications also found in the cult-legal priestly texts.

Yet the phrase לכפר עליו in Lev 1:4bβ is by far too ambiguous for the assumption of a radical reconceptualization of the עלה tradition as expressed by Elliger. What remains, therefore, is the understanding of the עלה concept in Lev 1:3–9 in its traditional sense but including the aspect of expiation for sin in a wider sense, and with it the meaning of v. 9bβ in the sense that the pleasant odor of the עלה is either to please or to appease Yahweh.

2. Indirect signals

There are also indirect signals in the unified prescription of the procedure which reveal the conceptual specificness of the עלה. One of those signals is basic, and three others qualify the basic one in particular respects.

Basic to the total prescription is the perception that the procedure moves consistently forward from its very beginning, presumably at the offerer's home place away from the sanctuary, to its conclusion up to the fiery consumption of the whole animal, to the stage where − leaving offerer and priest behind − the fire itself takes over the animal "caused" by the priest to burn. Nothing less, yet no thing more either!

This basic perception is complemented by the specific aspects. One of these aspects was mentioned earlier. It is indicated by the ever-narrowing of the envisioned procedure, from the broad קרבן system, via those sacrificial stages which the עלה shares with other sacrifices, to those that focus on the עלה specifically and again specifically to those that involve an ox. This narrowing of the systemic aspect which shows the עלה as specifically evolving within the total קרבן system, the system of sacrificial bringing near to Yahweh, includes the ever-narrowing of the procedure's territorial perspective. This is true especially when seen from the vantage point of the altar toward which the animal is moved: from the territory of the land to the territory of the sanctuary (its entrance) to the place of slaughter and to the altar.

The second aspect is indicated by the transfer of the animal from the hands of the offerer away from the altar to the hands of the priest at the altar, an indispensable qualitative specification in the animal's rite of passage without which the offerer's objective cannot be implemented.

Last, and perhaps most important, the עלה ox is processed in a steadily upward movement. This interpretation is based on the imagery reflected by the text, indeed on some of its direct signals, irrespective of whether or not the noun עלה is derived from the verb עלה. We have earlier suggested that the entire apodosis of the case law, focusing on an עלה-gift, presupposes the offerer's pilgrimage, a מעלה from his home place up to the sanctuary. The sanctuary, certainly the one legitimate sanctuary in Jerusalem, is literally a high place. At the sanctuary, the animal is either killed while it lies on the floor (so with Rendtorff) or killed while it stands before it collapses to the floor whence the blood and its pieces are successively lifted up and taken upward to the altar. Here the blood is tossed against its base (it does not go up to Yahweh) and the pieces lifted upon (על) the pyramid of wood-pieces which are upon (על) the fire which is upon (על) the altar (vv. 7b, 8), the top of which is high and must be reached either by steps or (because of Exod 20:25f.) by a ramp whence, finally, the whole animal is by the priest caused to smoke on the altar,[63] i.e., to be transformed into smoke that rises in pleasant odor straight upward to Yahweh[64] so that he may be pleased or appeased and react accordingly.

The final station in the animal's rite of passage, referred to in v. 9bα and β, is particularly important. It not only prescribes the priest's concluding act that sums up the whole procedure, but it also conceptually marks the decisive moment of transition in the animal's rite of passage. This passage does not come to its conclusion with the completion of the

---

[63] המזבחה, ה locale; cf. grammars; R. RENDTORFF (1985: 60).

[64] The smoke is scarcely thought of as turning sideways toward the tabernacle, its holy of holies, or toward the place of the deity's revelation in front of it. The perception of its upward direction reveals its originality which is independent of the imagery of the holy of holies or the sanctuary as Yahweh's dwelling place.

actants' activities. Conceptually, it continues, which shows that the human actants are serving the animal's rite of passage by their own actions.

The priest "causes" the whole "to smoke," הקטיר, v. 9bα.[65] He does not burn or smoke it himself. He only starts that process. With that function his activities end, whereas the animal's rite of passage goes on into its final motion. Strictly speaking, the priest does not even cause the animal to smoke. He only causes it to burn. It is the fire itself that from now on becomes the procedural agent (cf. אש mentioned three times in vv. 7 and 8). Through the fire, the already killed animal is subjected to its second decisive transformation: a transformation into smoke. Thus, it goes up to Yahweh as smoke. And what counts at its arrrival at Yahweh is not the atmospheric quality of the smoke (v. 9b), but the aesthetic quality of the smoke — its pleasant odor. One can observe how the terminology for fire (אש) and smoke (הקטיר and ריח־ניחוח) successively used as the text progresses, is accompanied by or is based on (if not expressive of) the conceptuality of the progressive transformation of the animal in its rite of passage. One also observes that in this rite, not even the smoke, let alone the fire, is useful unless the odor is pleasant.[66] One can also observe that v. 9bα and β are related not only syntactically but also, and especially, conceptually in semantically progressive aspects to the effect that v. 9bβ, while expressing the decisive notion of pleasant odor, points nevertheless to nothing more than the end station of the animal's procedure, of its rite of passage. These observations coincide with what has earlier been concluded about the meaning of the phrase אשה ריח־ניחזח ליהוה: that, notwithstanding its connoted purposive function, it refers to a gift for Yahweh which has a pleasant odor. As that pleasant odor, it arrives at Yahweh. And it cannot achieve more than an intention to be accepted by Yahweh with favor, not even in the final motion of its passage after the priest and, even more, the offerer are left behind having motioned the gift through their own procedures. Their prescribed procedures point to the sacrificial object's own procedure,

---

[65] B. LEVINE translates: "The priest shall turn the whole into smoke," and explains: "The burned parts of the victim rise *as smoke* when they are consumed by the altar fire" (7, emphasis mine). This interpretation comes close. Clearer still is that the priest causes the whole to turn into smoke, because it is the fire that turns the animal into smoke, not the priest. Levine's explanation confirms this understanding indirectly: the "burned parts" which rise as smoke — "in transmuted form" (6) — are burned by the fire, אש. In what sense is the animal a "victim"? Cf. n.40 above.

[66] B. LEVINE (6): "The sacrifice, in its transmuted form, reaches God." Exactly!

and beyond their own activities to its final upward movement until it arrives at Yahweh as a pleasant odor.[67]

Excursus: The altar

The altar is mentioned in vv. 5bβ, 7a, 8b, 9bα. It is the indispensable instrument via which the offerer's sacrifice can be launched onto its way to the deity. Directly connected with this notion is the aspect of either the elevated place of altars or their own height. Altars are meaningfully built structures. An altar could be, but is not, built as a fire-pit. The aspect of the elevation or height of altars depends on sacral and not on practical necessities. It is governed by their function to provide access for the humans on earth to the deity in the heights. Their structure or place serves, therefore, as a vehicle for procedural motions in which sacrifices are moved upward to the deity — so much so that the offerers themselves are ultimately left behind while their sacrifice instead is transmitted from the altar through the fire to the deity. The altar does not only have a certain location and structure. Its location and structure have a specific function in the motion of the sacrificial procedure. They serve the conceptuality of that procedure.

The aspect of elevation is, therefore, intrinsic to the reality of existing altars. Its imagery is not abstract. It is the conceptual matrix for, rather than an abstracted perception independent of, real altars. The interpretation of this imagery is an exegetical necessity if one wants to understand the conceptuality — in our case — of a text concerned with sacrifice. Exegetically, the reference in the text to the altar cannot be passed by as a reference to a negligible piece of furniture, as if any such piece were negligible.

However, our text is not bound by the assumption of one specific altar structure. Its prescriptive, future oriented perspective must be taken to include the approximately six foot high altar for the desert sanctuary prescribed in Exod 27:1−8, although this altar scarcely serves the conditions for the sacrifices of oxen; cf. M. Noth: "Die angegebenen Maße

---

[67] B. LEVINE explains perceptively: "The offering may have been called *'olah* because its flames and smoke 'ascended' to heaven.... There was the 'ascent' of the sacrifice itself onto the altar, and one speaks of 'raising up' the *'olah*.... There is also the 'ascent' of the priest or the officiant or the donor onto a raised platform where the offering was to be made" (5, also 6). Our converging interpretations were made independently.

sind merkwürdig gering," and "die Frage wird nicht gestellt ob solche Konstruktion die Hitze beim Verbrennen von tierischem Opfer aushalten kann" (1959: 180). Yet the prescription looks beyond the altar of the desert time. Its only criterion is the עלה altar of the one legitimate "central" sanctuary. The different measurements given in Exod 27:1ff.; Ezek 43:13−17; II Chron 4 (cf. also II Kings 16:10−16 about "the great altar") are therefore of relative importance for the question of the sacrificial function of any of these altars.

3. Conclusions

Lev 1:3−9 operates on a number of diverse conceptual presuppositions. The reconstruction of these presuppositions is important because they reveal many aspects of the sacrificial system that are operative but not explicated in the next. They reveal the dimension of *Geistesbeschäftigung* in the text's focus on the actions themselves. This reconstruction becomes particularly important as an exegetical mechanism by which the discernment of the text's uniqueness against its conceptual background can be approached. The reconstruction of those concepts behind the text, e.g., for the purpose of our systematized understanding of its worldview, is certainly legitimate. But it serves that purpose and not the exegesis of texts. The reconstruction of presuppositions for the purpose of a better understanding of the uniqueness of a text itself serves quite a different objective. A set or system of presuppositions does not yet explain why a text says what it says and is what it is.

There can be no doubt that many of the conceptual aspects found in our text only elucidate specific parts of the text, while others point to the unity of the text. The conceptual aspects reveal the text's coherence, not only its cohesion. That coherence must be explained.

Lev 1:3−9 is עלה-בקר specific. However its genre is defined, it is confined not to ritual in general but to the עלה ritual in particular, and on this basis to the עלה of an ox or steer or bull. To this extent, it is imbedded in and determined by a generic typicality, a subgenre of prescriptions about rituals for sacrificial gifts of offerings. But as much as one can attempt to reconstruct, hypothetically and in abstraction, a generic structure underneath our text as its matrix, one has not yet explained its individual, textual structure. And that individuality is what we have to begin with in each case before us.

The individuality of our text is not explained by separate attention to each of its parts or sentences or verbs, although their inclusion is indispensable for the interpretation of their relationship and of the text as an entity. Their relationship reveals the text's coherence.

Attention to the individuality of the text does not presume its literary originality. It must keep in mind the possibilty of conflated literary layers, the fact that our text stands at the beginning of larger literary compositions, the differences in the עלה texts themselves (Lev 1:3−9, 10−13, 14−17), and also the fact of redactional frameworks and expansions (as in v. 4bβ, 3bβ, 4bα?), or changes (as from "the priest" in 9bα [MT] to the Aaronide "priests" in vv. 5b, 7a + b, 8aα). This specific redactional change may indicate more than a conceptual shift from one to several priests involved in the same ritual act, or to one at a time from among those of the Aaronides. The reference to the "priest" in v. 9bα, the (one) priest who completes the procedure, besides the reference to the "priests" concerned with the blood-rite and the setting for the fire, may point to the distinction in the text as it evolved in its redaction history between a main priest and a supporting priestly cast involved in the same ritual procedure. It may reflect a post-deuteronomic development in which the Levitic priests either remain qualified as priests by virtue of their Aaronide descent and under the supervision of a main priest, now from a different Aaronide lineage, or a development in which the Levitic priests are on the way to being replaced as priests by priests from that different Aaronide lineage in an emerging priestly hierarchic structure within that lineage. These possibilities find support in the different distributions of work: the priests do subsidiary, auxiliary work, at the altar, whereas the main (not yet the high, הכהן הגדול) priest functions at the completion of the whole sacrifice.

The signals contained in the individual sentences include references to and aspects of the actants, the sacrificial object, the instruments, places, and synchronic as well as diachronic order. The thirteen actions indicated by the verbs dominate the other aspects because they point to the distinctiveness of each step of the procedure more than any other indicator. Above all, they point to the procedure itself, and to the question of the coherence of the thirteen actions in it.

The way in which the verbs function in the text, individually and in relation to one another, deserves special attention. Individually, they are used in a twofold sense. They characterize an action without de-

scribing how it is to be performed; and they refer to the totality of an
action that consists of more than one act by expressing only one of those
acts.

For example, the verb שׁחט in v. 5 a does not describe how the slaughter
is to be done, namely, by cutting the animal's throat. In view of alternative possibilities for killing an animal, this amounts to an interesting
absence of descriptive accuracy. This absence is not simply explained by
saying that the knowledge of the specific mode of slaughter is not worth
mentioning because it is presupposed, especially if that mode must be
observed in contradistinction to other available modes. The specific
mode of slaughter is certainly important, and its prescription should be
expected. Why is such a prescription absent? This question can only be
sufficiently answered if we assume that the actual prescription to
"slaughter" does not mean something besides or in addition to the mode
of slaughter, something that would be important whereas the mode itself
would be irrelevant, but that it means the necessary mode itself. While
not referring to the mode *of* slaughter, the formulated prescription
refers to that very mode *as* "slaughter." The verb characterizes and
qualifies the *nature* of the killing and of the required mode of its execution. The killing is "slaughter."

Furthermore, the verb שׁחט not only denotes the specific act of slaugh-
tering, is also connotes at least one subsidiary action, the taking up of a
knife. In this, as in other cases in the text, the verb has a *pars pro toto*
function. It signifies the total activity while only expressing a part of it.

Last but not least, the verb שׁחט functions in relation to the other verbs
in the text, directly in relation to the ritual meaning of סמך יד in v. 4, and
especially in relation to bringing the animal's blood and sprinkling it on
the altar in v. 5b. It is specifically predicated in the fact that the killed
animal's blood must not be spilled on the ground, as in Deut 12:16 and
I Sam 14:32. Apart from this fact, the animal could be killed in alternative ways in order to be burned on the altar. Its slaughter is assumed to
happen in consideration of the requirement that its blood be spared for
the altar. The usage of the verb in v. 5a anticipates the statements in v.
5bα and β.

With respect to the distinctions in perspective, what has been said
about שׁחט in v. 5a could also be said about the actions expressed by the
other verbs in the text. These verbs characterize particular actions rather
than specifically describing them. Each signifies the totality of an action
that consists of more than the specific act denoted by them. Just as they

express these individual actions in their particular characterizing and holistic perspective, they are perceived in light of the function of these actions in the progress of the whole procedure. Whatever subsidiary actions are presupposed (and presupposed to be important), the absence of their explication is caused by the focus on what is decisive, in the individual actions, for the ritual goal of the whole procedure. The verbs and the sentences depend on their focus on this goal, and they are selected and expressed in light of it. In their individual expessions and in their coordination, they reflect the result of a systematic understanding of the meaning and goal of the forward-moving progression of the procedure. This understanding is itself the presupposition for the concise expressions of the prescriptions and for the compactness of the total text.

If the forward-moving progression of the procedure is the basic aspect for the coherence of what is prescribed, it is understandable that the surface text does not differentiate between main and subsidiary sacrificial actions *(Haupt- und Nebenhandlungen)*, between thirteen individual actions and nine stages, between preparations and ritual proper, between different sacrificial qualities of even some main acts − expect for the obvious differences between offerer and priest − and between synchronic and diachronic order. The text itself wants to make sure that the procedure moves forward to its completion so that its purpose may be fulfilled. When seen in this light, none of the prescribed steps may be missing. Each is equally important. And more are not necessary. Indeed, the importance of the prescriptions for the so-called *Nebenhandlungen* becomes once more understandable in this light.[68] *We should conclude that the structure of the text is governed by the perspective of the steps typically qualified for securing the movement of the עלה-בקר procedure toward its completion,* notwithstanding the fact that those steps take place successively or simultaneously, at different places, and involve the different actions and persons. Ultimately, *the text's structure is determined by its focus on the goal of the completed ritual itself.*

---

[68] The interpretation of the text's interest in the *rite* performance is problematic. A prescription for *rite* performance would, on the one hand, most probably have to distinguish explicitly between *Haupt- und Nebenhandlungen* − which the text does not do − and, on the other hand, have to be more specific in prescribing *how* some of these actions must be performed, rather than just *that* they must be performed. Yet we may say that the text is interested in *rite* performance in as much as it prescribes those essential steps that were necessary for the forward-moving progression of the procedure toward the completion of the ritual and the achievement of its purpose − if *"rite"* can be defined in this way.

The text prescribes what must be done. Yet as much as it determines the acts and the pattern for the ritual enactment, it aims at more than the practical implementation of verbal instructions. Its predominant perspective does not lie in the emphasis that words must be followed by actions and that words become valid and effective only when enacted – as if only actions count, regardless of what is done and for what reasons. The predominant perspective in the prescription is guided instead by the purpose and goal of the ritual to be enacted. This goal is to secure the ritual's purpose in its enactment. It presupposes the tradition of עלה enactments and their purpose. The text does not introduce a new type of sacrifice. It only regulates the procedure of the well-known and practiced tradition of עלה sacrifices so that their purpose may be accomplished. The text's own prescription is subservient to the purpose of the actual עלה sacrifices. This fact is above all indicated by the interpretive elements in the text, elements that interpret the ritual acts, partly directly in vv. 3bβ, 4bα + β, 9bβ, and partly indirectly as in the phrases "for Yahweh" and "before Yahweh," vv. 2aβ, 4bβ, 5a, 9bβ. It is also indicated in the terminological shifts from the zoological classification (בקר) of the sacrificial object to its functional denotation as עלה, vv. 4a, 6a, 9bβ, and from the atmospheric to the aesthetic aspects in the עלה-animal's transformation during the final stage of its rite of passage. It is furthermore indicated by conceptual aspects in the *ductus* of the text, especially those involving the process of an ever-narrowing and increasingly sacred territory, of the transition from offerer to priest, and of the ever-upward-processing of the עלה itself, finally up to Yahweh. *The prescription rests on the conceptuality of the necessary procedure for the transmission of the עלה-animal through its final and total fiery consumption as a gift for Yahweh, so that it will reach Yahweh in order that he may, for the offerer's sake, be pleased or appeased by its pleasant odor.*

§15 The genre of the text

1. The discussion about "Ritual"

The question of genre has been a particular crux in the interpretation of the text-type to which our text belongs. The discussion was prompted by, and has centered around, R. Rendtorff's original contention that there is a group of texts which belong to a literary genre "Ritual." This genre, a particular subgenre of J. Begrich's priestly *Da'at* (דעת) which Begrich had not observed when defining his *Da'at,* is according to Rendtorff characterized by short verbal sentences in the impersonal third person and perf. consecutive style which prescribed the individual sacrificial acts, and which are combined to form literary units in which the successive course of the sacrificial procedures is prescribed in its entirety. It is characterized by a concluding formula as well.

The genre "Ritual" is said to be constituted by literary compositions which evolved from the originally short oral declarations identified by Begrich. Traditio-historically, it represents a transformation from the orality of the genre "Priestly *Da'at*" to a genuinely literary genre. This transformation reflects the final stage in the development of the sacrificial cult.[69] And contrary to the short phrases of the original oral *Da'at* which were meant for the professional instruction of the priests, Rendtorff's texts of the *Da'at* genre "Ritual" were designated for public delivery. They were no "inner-priestly" writings.[70] They aimed at, rather than resulted from, oral delivery. In the relationship between orality and literature, they mark a shift in development from literature out of orality to orality out of literature.

Rendtorff's identification of his genre "Ritual" proved to be very seminal, but also controversial in the discussion. While some supported and built on it, such as K. Koch in *Die Priesterschrift,* others rejected it. It was initially contested by K. Elliger (30−31), subsequently by an

---

[69] R. Rendtorff (1954: 77).
[70] R. Rendtorff (1954: 12, 77).

increasing chorus, and most lately by B. Janowski (194, 328–333).[71] Most recently, Rendtorff has abandoned the literary-critical and syntactical distinctions that formed part of the basis for his original identification of the generic "Ritual"-texts. Yet he has nevertheless upheld his position on the genre itself with reference to their characteristic formulaic *Ritualstil* (1985: 19). This defense is not persuasive, for reasons other than those already offered in our own study.

If literary critical distinctions for the reconstruction of an original "Ritual," in characteristic formulaic style, must be ruled out, the basis for its identification can only be found in the structure and in the characteristic style of the text at hand. And if the texts at hand are stylistically and syntactically variable or mixed – which is more or less the case in the many texts of the genre, however defined – the identification of a genre "Ritual" must show why it rests on the characteristic *waw* perf. impersonal style rather than on the stylistic variability of its texts. As long as it rests on that criterion alone, it presupposes either an original text, i.e., a literary critical judgment, or a stylistic ideal in which the generic nature of a text existing in its totality is reduced to the text's characteristic stylistic features as the criterion for determining its genre. The question arises, however, whether a particular style alone constitutes a genre. A typical style belongs to a genre, but does not constitute it, at least not alone. It may be germane to an author, a literary school, or a literary work which employs it for different genres. Style criticism plays a role in but is not identical with genre criticism. The same is true for texts in poetry and prose, and also for the style of many texts in the priestly corpus. While genres have characteristic stylistic features, they also are stylistically variable. Both phenomena together contribute to pointing to a genre, but until additional factors are considered, a genre cannot be determined by those phenomena alone.

To be sure, the difference between the prescriptions in third and second person form must not be overlooked. But unless the genre "Ritual" is identified by this difference alone – which is not the case and would be insufficient anyway because the third person style belongs to the repertoire of the case law language – one has to take into account

---

[71] For the latest listing of the opposing authors and a summary of their arguments, see B. Janowski (328). Regardless of whether one agrees with Rendtorff or not, it should be noted that the controversial discussion about his thesis has not captured the full range of aspects addressed and implied in his *Die Gesetze,* especially in form-critical and traditio-historical respects.

not only the perfect and inverted imperfect constructions and the succession of prescriptions but also the different subjects with which the units are concerned, and their respective settings. Indeed, Rendtorff's own determination of the genre "Ritual" depend as much, if not essentially, on his focus on the subject of sacrifices and the institution of the sacrificial cult (1954: 12, 77) as it depends on a generic style. And surely, a genre "Ritual" would be identifiable in the texts under discussion only because they are concerned with rituals for sacrifices, because they presuppose the tradition of actual sacrifices ritually performed. It would be a "Sacrifice-Ritual" which would be constituted by the prescription for sacrificial procedures. In Rendtorff's discussion, the genre "Ritual" would not exist without sacrifices as its decisive point of reference; it is explicitly and specifically connected with that subject. It is virtually certain that he would not have identified it without this connection, which is itself based on the traditions of priestly activities involving *Da'at* and instruction of *Da'at,* rather than simply on the basis of the characteristic style of the texts.[72]

Still more is at stake. The German word *Ritualstil* used for the texts about the sacrifices implies that this style is generically characteristic only for the prescriptions of sacrificial procedures, an obviously indefensible proposition. The style is used, among other things, for prescriptions other than ritual sacrificial procedures, for statements of facts or conditions in or apart from procedures, and particularly — if only mostly in the second person perf. form because Moses is addressed personally — in the prescriptions for the construction of the sanctuary and its accessories. The style is certainly characteristic and, for the pericopes, formulaic. But unless one subsumes everything for which it is used under "Ritual," one cannot call it *Ritualstil.* It is employed, but not exclusively, for the prescriptions *of* sacrifice-rituals. But it does not constitute the criterion for a genre "Ritual."[73]

What has been said ought also to be considered in light of the issue of rituals in general. We should grant that the word "ritual" may be used for an actual ritual procedure but also for a prescriptive formulary for such a

---

[72] M. Noth calls it "ein Opferritual" (1962: 11), apparently in Rendtorff's sense (and probably influenced by him) of a literary genre, and with the clear reference to that about which the offerer must be informed, yet Noth does not refer to the style of the "Ritual."

[73] K. Elliger speaks of an "Überspitzung des Prinzips vom Stilzwang der Gattung" (31).

procedure.[74] One may have to decide from case to case whether a given text should be defined as Ritual generically or as a generically otherwise-identifiable description or prescription of, or reference to, an actual ritual performance. In either case, "ritual" is constituted by the order of the procedure, "die *Handlungs*ordnung," while the style in which this order is expressed may vary. And more than by style, the different procedural patterns are determined by their typical occasions, as the Old Testament alone demonstrates in its references to, among others, rituals of enthrone-ment, of seasonal celebrations, of "rites of passage," of diverse cultic procedures, of dedications of persons and sanctuaries, etc. The discussion of ritual for or of sacrifice cannot be isolated from these considerations.

2. Prescription of ritual, as case law

If it appears too difficult to rationalize a genre "Ritual" for the prescriptions of sacrificial procedures on the ground of *Ritualstil*, we must consider an alternative option for the generic identification of the priestly texts concerned with sacrifice, and also of Lev 1:2 aβ + b and 3−9: the genre of the case laws themselves. It has long been recognized that the texts about sacrifices in the priestly corpus reflect the case law pattern according to which not only individual laws are structured but entire collections of laws are composed. And it has been recognized that Lev 1−5 belongs to this pattern.[75] The problem is that these observations have fallen under the category of "casuistic framework," which in our cases presupposes the redaction-critical judgment no longer relevant for the consideration of genre.

---

[74] B. JANOWSKI's preference for the science of religion definition of a ritually fixed course of action, *"ein rituell festgelegter Handlungsablauf,"* sides with ritual as actual procedure. However, the fixed format of such procedure points to the prior act or tradition of fixation, or of its understanding as fixed, and, thus, to the distinction between fixation and actualization. It therefore allows for the utilization of the word "ritual" for either the fixation or the actualization of the *Handlungsablauf*. As a term for fixation, the word would denote a genre, whereas it would denote the setting of the applied genre when applied for the actual performance.

[75] For convenient references see G. LIEDKE (22−35, 96f.). The latest author who points to this fact is B. LEVINE who says that the כי clause in v. 2 aβ "is the sign of the casuistic formulation so characteristic of biblical and ancient Near Eastern law codes" (4−5). That the same is true for the אם clause in v. 3 aα and that the Punic so-called "tariffs" illustrate the similarities to the laws in Leviticus "substantively" and "in composition and formulation" is noted as well.

R. Rendtorff states that the complex Lev 1−5 "ist eingespannt in den kasuistischen Rahmen" (1954: 11): "der kasuistisch formulierte Rahmen" (1967: 8). The opening statements in his *Leviticus* under *"Form"* (17) refer only to the main case, *"Hauptfall,"* and the subdivision(s), *"Untergliederung,"* while a reference to the framework, *"Rahmen,"* is missing and the exegesis proceeds from the short discussion of the macro-composition directly to the acts of the sacrificial procedure and its *Ritualstil* (18).

K. Koch (1959: 5ln.5) speaks about "den Versuch einer kasuistischen Ordnung" which is, however, undercut by the order of the *Rituale* in Exod 25ff., a problematic assumption for that corpus unless the important distinction between the prescriptions for the one-time building of the sanctuary (as a ritual sacrificial performance?) and the prescriptions for each and every case of a particular sacrifice are declared irrelevant. On p. 100, Koch pays attention to this distinction and explains that P has with respect to the repetitiveness of the sacrificial act "Lv. 1ff. mit einem besonderen Rahmen ausgestaltet und dieser Rahmen ist dem kasuistischen Recht *nachgebildet"* (emphasis mine); but it is possible "diese Reihen aus dem jetzigen Zusammenhang herauszuschälen" (1959: 97) − which happens through literary-critical judgments and, depending on Rendtorff's classification, also on a presumed originally independent layer of a genre "Ritual." Even if that were the case, why should we speak about *imitation* of case law rather than the *transformation* of a genre Ritual into the genre of case law, precisely for P's reasons stated on p. 100? Indeed, Koch speaks on p. 99 (p. 96 according to Liedke's reference to it: 31n.3) about *"den Wandel der Gattungen beim Übergang von der mündlichen zur schriftlichen Überlieferung"* (emphasis his). This seems to be the case. But it would be clearer if we would say that a transformation of genres means the adaptation or transfer of texts from one genre into or by a different, even an established, genre, rather than their generic disintegration into a genre imitation now indicated as framework. It may be added that for both Rendtorff and Koch, the *Rituale* existed independently as written texts before their integration into the redactional framework. However, while Rendtorff has maintained that they represent a genuinely literary genre that originated in literary activities, Koch has said that the written *Rituale* originated as a genre of oral instruction.

M. Noth (1962: 12), while noting literary critical observations, sidesteps explicit reference to a *Rahmen,* and says instead that "mit v. 2b [sic! he means 2 aβ + b] beginnt der eigentliche Ritual-Text," which presupposes his identification of this text on the generic basis of case law, even for P except for the secondary word קרבן. And he interprets the structural aspects with reference to his interpretation of the case laws in his Exodus commentary. Thus, while saying "Opferritual" (11), Noth seems at the same time to indicate that his *Opferritual* belongs to the genre of case law.

K. Elliger (28), assuming a *Vorlage* which as for Noth had עלה instead of קרבן in v. 2 aβ + b, offers a hypothetical text for that *Vorlage* which contains the protasis of v. 2 aβ and amounts therefore to the case law genre at the outset, although Elliger does not say it.

Finally, G. Liedke (37) says: "Es fällt auf, daß in Dtn und besonders in P und Qumran die qatal-x-Form gegenüber x-yiqtol stark in den Vordergrund tritt, während sich im BB und in H beide Formulierungen etwa die Waage halten. Das Überwiegen der qatal-x-Form in P kommt durch die Aufnahme von <Ritualen> in viele Nachsätze zustande.[2] [footnote referring to Rendtorff, 1954: 12; Koch, 1959: 8] Diese Gattung ist gerade durch die <stereotypen kurzen Verbalsätze> in der <unpersönlichen 3. pers. sing. und im perf. cons.>[3] [footnote referring to Rendtorff, 1954: 12] gekennzeichnet." Why do the qatal-x-forms point to *Ritualen* only in P and not also in Deut? Liedke's interpretation rests on and accepts the results of Rendtorff's definition of that *Gattung* on the basis of P alone as an established conclusion, or he could not have said what he said while still confining this form to a genre "Ritual." And Rendtorff comes close to giving the impression that Liedke's position has confirmed his own results (1985: 19). If Rendtorff's "Ritual" does not stand up, Liedke has no basis for his position.

If the literary-critical criteria for dissociating the protases in our text(s) from an older layer contained in its/their apodoses are set aside or, more importantly, prove to be invalid, the designation of the protases in these texts as "framework" is indefensible, and the protases must themselves be considered as intrinsic elements of the text's generic identity, as elements of genuine case laws. This is indeed the basic form of these texts. Thus, in addition to the strong questionability – at least – of a genre "Ritual" apart from the protases in the texts at hand, we must account for their current case law-genre form, and for a tradition- and transmission-historical picture in which the current case laws did not evolve from "Rituals" but in which the case law-genre, available from the traditions of noncultic law, was adopted by priests into their cultic

setting for the prescription of particular cases of cultic laws, both substantive and procedural and especially for sacrificial procedures. That
apparently happened in a style that was fitting, if not to a specific time, to
particular groups of writers and their stylistic tradition, and that lent
itself for the subjects to be prescribed. For the time being, this interpretation of the genre of our texts, including Lev 1:2aβ + b and 3–9, is
preferable because it accounts for the text-units directly, can be explained tradition- and transmission-historically, and is less burdened
with questionable presuppositions. *Our texts belong to the genre of case
law; specifically, case law concerning the ritual procedure for sacrifices.*

§ 16 The purpose and setting of the text

What is the purpose of the text?[76] While certainty in this question is even less likely than in all the other questions, we can still ponder the lower or higher degrees of possibility.

1. Instruction?

The prevailing common denominator in the scholarly discussion is that the prescriptions serve instruction *(Unterrichtung, Belehrung)* especially for lay people. The main argument advanced in favor of instruction is the concise form of the text suited for teaching and learning, and the lay person's need to know what he has to do and what he has to leave to the priest. This argument seems to be supported by the framework formula 1:2 aα, Yahweh's command to Moses to speak (the following) to the Israelites. This argument is relative.

The Yahweh-commands to Moses presuppose instruction about all sorts of subjects and in quite a variety of forms and genres. To that extent, everything said within these frameworks is instruction for the Israelites which Moses received and was commanded to pass on to them. The argument proves only that laws can be instructed, too, but not that the purpose of their creation, their formulation and composition, is for instruction, let alone for instruction only.

Specifically, the Yahweh command to Moses in Lev 1:2 aα commands instruction about all types and subtypes of the sacrificial gifts listed in chapters 1–3, rather than only one at a time. It assumes instruction about a major part of the sacrificial system, and instruction by Moses at Sinai once and for all for all Israelites both priests and lay persons, rather than instruction for lay persons by priests. In the present context of the Yahweh speech to Moses, the case law prescriptions are − so we may

---

[76] For a summary of the arguments, see R. RENDTORFF (1985: 21), who correctly says that "wir werden in dieser Frage über Vermutungen nicht hinauskommen."

interpret the hermeneutic of their transmission history — instructions for all Israelites in the sense of the authentic origin of the sacrificial system, and in the sense that the written Torah-text of the priests is read to the Israelites wherever and whenever the Torah is read.

This instructional scenario differs markedly from a setting in which a specific procedural prescription, as in the case of Lev 1:3–9, could serve for the instruction of an individual offerer in the particular situation of his offering. And it is not coincidental that this scenario has played no relevant role in the argument in favor of lay instruction.

When taking a prescription of procedure, such as 1:3–9, in isolation, it is equally problematic to assume that its main, let alone sole, purpose was instruction. The impersonal third person style, as well as the general focus in the protasis on anyone who brings such an offering is characteristic for the procedure. The text does not address instructees directly in second person style. In contrast to forms of direct instruction, it instructs at best indirectly. It is neither instruction *ad personam* nor *ad personas*. It is issue or procedure oriented by tying a person, an individual, into the procedure rather than by applying the procedure to an individual. It speaks about the same procedure for one person among all persons.

Applied as instruction to any specific sacrificial situation which is envisioned by the text, the *ductus* of the procedure would have to be transformed, presumably by a priest who instructs the offerer directly, saying, "This is what you must do." Such a transformed personal application in a specific situation is inevitable even if the text is read to or by an offerer before he is told or tells himself that, therefore, he must act as the law just told him. To whatever extent the text is supposed to be instruction *ad personam* in actual sacrificial cases, it is distanced from direct instructional situations.

What has just been said is supported by the fact that the text speaks about the priest's as well as about the offerer's role. There is no longer a reason for assuming an original text according to which the sole sacrificial actant was the offerer. Indeed, one of the traditio-historical implications in the text may well be to make clear the role reserved solely for the priests. M. Noth's suggestion (1962: 11) in support of the theory of lay instruction, that the offerer must know the difference between his and the priest's activities, is not persuasive. Why should it be the text's purpose to explicitly instruct the offerer about what must be self-explanatory for him, especially in the presence of the priest(s): that he has no business with the actions at the altar? The text speaks about the actions of both the priest and the offerer in the sacrificial procedure. And just as it is not direct instruction to the offerer, it is not direct instruction − even less so − to the priest.

The undifferentiated assumption of instruction intended especially for lay persons also becomes relativized when one ponders the prescriptions themselves. Much as they state what the participants have to do, they do not describe all activities exactly or specifically. But even with respect to what they do express, one has to ask why the participants should have to be instructed about these essential acts, precisely because the prescriptions are so few and focused on the typical in the activities. The priest has no need at all to be instructed about his role before each participation in an עלה. He knows his six acts because he performs them all the time. And why should the offerer be explicitly instructed about his, at most, seven acts? When he decides (at home!) to bring a type of עלה, בקר or צאן or עוף, he must know about the condition of the animal to be selected before he may receive any instruction at the sanctuary for its sacrifice. And he must know before that sacrifice that he has to bring his ox to the sanctuary. Yet the apodosis includes the prescriptions for bringing the selected ox to the sanctuary, too. Should the individual benefit from the instruction, which is a necessary presupposition for this assumption of the text's purpose, the text definitely would have to presuppose separate instructional occasions or settings, one apart from any actual sacrifice at the sanctuary even before the offerer decides on bringing a sacrifice, and another that would instruct him at the beginning of the sacrificial proce- dure after he has arrived at the sanctuary's entrance. The text in its apodosis form already indicates no such instructional distinctions. And since what is said in the apodosis depends on the perspective expressed in the protasis, that perspective indicates the offerer's situation to which the total case law refers. In its total form, its claimed instructional purpose, including the instructions about his acts at the sanctuary, would have to be implemented in situations or settings before and apart from his pilgrimage. If the case law is lay instruction, not only the form but also the setting of such instruction is indeed very distanced from the general setting and the specific situation of any sacrificial procedure.

Still more is at stake. If instruction is supposed to take place in conjunction with the sacrificial procedure, it can only refer to the five acts of the offerer stated in vv. 4a, 5a, 6a + b, 9a. Apart from the fact that such an understanding would again presuppose a textbase stripped

of its case law form, one would have to ask why the offerer would have
to read the instruction concerning his five acts, or have them read to
him. When bringing his עלה (doesn't he know that he brings an עלה?)
to the sanctuary, he may have to be informed about his initial act of
pressing down firmly with his hand, but does he have to be explicitly
instructed that he must kill, skin, dissect the animal, and wash its
entrails? Has not tradition taught him so? It seems that our assumptions of the instructional purpose or intention of the texts about the
sacrifices are inherited more from a general perception of Torah as
instruction than from observations of their specific nature. We must
look for alternative options.

2. Prescription for procedure

A number of aspects are basic and cannot be overlooked. One aspect
highlights the text's emphasis on the sacrificial procedure. It is supported by the issue-oriented perspective implied in the usage of the
third person sing. form. Another aspect points to the prescriptive nature of the text, which presupposes potential cases in the future for
which the prescription serves. We have also argued that the text belongs to the genre of case law, the function of which is in our instance to
lay down objectively the rules for the procedure of the particular עלה-
בקר sacrifice. In addition to these observations, two other important
aspects must be mentioned: the genuinely literary nature of the text,
and the specific fact that it is part of an original literary composition.

The assumption that our text, and its related texts, may be the written record of an originally oral text lacks sufficient substantiation. R.
Rendtorff's original claim in his 1954 *Gesetze* that even his *Rituale* were
genuinely written creations for the purpose of oral delivery rather than
written copies of originally oral texts remains fundamentally valid. But
we must now assume that our text was genuinely written in the case law
genre. It is genuine cult-legal literature. And it did not exist as an
originally independent pericope. Whatever compositional shifts can be
observed, caused by redactors, our pericope must be considered as part
of an original literary body which comprised clusters of typically related
case laws about types and subtypes of sacrifices and which possibly
existed before its inclusion into the Sinai pericope. Of that original
body, Lev 1:2aβ + b must have been an introductory part, either for

the collection of a קרבן or for an עלה cluster. Lev 1: 2 aβ + b is itself a case law which introduces all specific cases of its cluster.

Most important, however, especially for the question of a possible instructional purpose of this literary body, is the fact that this literary activity must have had its own specific setting. Whatever may be meant by instruction, it always requires an instructional setting. If an instructional setting is assumed for these laws, one will first have to ask whether such a setting would be identical with the setting in which the corpus was written, before one wonders whether its instruction coincided with actual sacrifices. The question is important because the discussion of the purpose of the laws may have something to do with the purpose of the setting in which they were written.

Strictly speaking, there is no evidence for the coincidence of a writing and an instructional setting, and its assumption is practically impossible. Even in a school, the activities of writers and of instructors, even should they involve identical persons, are separate and happen literally in different rooms and at successive times, quite apart from the basic fact that instruction involves modes of direct communication between instructor and present instructees while writing involves the writer with his script only. We must even assume that the writing and the sacrificing priests anticipated in the texts were not the same. The writing priests in their own setting wrote the prescriptions for the sacrificing priests, and not only for lay persons, in their sacrificial setting. They may have written − should the texts have originated during the first or second temple period − at or near the premises of the temple. They may! Even that is not certain. Yet whether they wrote during the time of one of the temples or during the exilic interim, they must have written the corpus before the sacrifices could be administered as prescribed even had they been identical with the sacrificing priests. They certainly did not write the corpus while participating in sacrifices. The genuinely literary nature of the composition of case laws, the literary activity of its writers in distinction to sacrificing priests, their place and time, all these factors point to a setting that is writing-specific, and in principle separate from the sacrificial setting on which they focus. Any discussion of the instructional purpose of this corpus will have to confront the question not only about the stylistic transformation of the texts from their case law form to a genuinely instructional form, i.e., about how the instruction was expressed to instructees, but also about where and when either the total corpus or any of its individual laws were transformed. It will have to account for the transposition of the laws from the genre and setting of their writing to the forms and setting of their instructional application. Even then, one has not yet confronted the primary question of the purpose of the setting itself in which the laws were written, and the alternatives when discussing the purpose either of law writing or of written laws. That purpose may have something to do with instruction. Yet, it may also, if not primarily, have to do with the clarification of the conditions for the sacrificial procedure, with the objectification of the procedure itself. Then, the question of the purpose of the law corpus would primarily involve the relationship of the written text to its ritual *implementation* rather than to the question of its instruction. And while R. Rendtorff has been correct in pointing out the genuinely literary nature of the corpus – an assumption with which we have to start – his other conclusion (and the *opinio communis* as well) that its laws were "zum öffentlichen Vortrag bestimmt" (1954: 77), as the definition of their primary or essential purpose, will have to be questioned in view of the alternative that they were primarily written to be so *implemented* by the public rather than to be publicly taught.

The fact that we have in Lev 1–3 or 1–5 or 1–7 clusters or procedural prescriptions for already known and presupposed traditional types of sacrifices, clusters that represent genuinely literary compositions, indicates that their literary production in writing settings must itself have (had) a purpose. This purpose should primarily be found in the conscious, conceptualized systematization of, ultimately, the total sacrificial cult, a systematization within which and on the basis of which the procedures for the individual sacrificial types and their subtypes can be clearly identified and demarcated from one another. It is not coincidental that every exegete realizes the systematized nature of this corpus at the outset, not just as it is positioned within the framework of the Sinai pericope, immediately following the establishment of the sanctuary. Its systematized nature is itself the fulfillment of a purpose that must be sought in the programmatic integration of the sacrificial traditions into a cultic sacrificial system of mutually differentiated types of sacrifices. Such integration requires a considered conceptualizing effort on the part of the priestly writers, whose programmatic tendencies pervade their entire work.[77] And it should not surprise us that it was composed both overall and in detail as a genuinely literary work.

---

[77] See K. Koch's assertion: "Was P schreibt, ist eine Programmschrift" (1959: 100).

According to what can be seen, this literary work represents a novelty in the history of Israel's rulings for sacrificial procedures.[78] It is an analogy, if not the analogy, to the literary nature of the systematized deuteronomic corpus, if only on the specifically cultic-sacrificial issues. The novelty of this literary phenomenon can scarcely be overestimated. One can to a certain extent reconstruct the history of Israel's sacrificial cult, as ,e.g., R. Rendtorff has done in his *Studien*. But where does one see a history of procedural prescriptions, orally or in writing, let alone systematized? Our literary corpus appears to respond to needs and tendencies, perhaps in view of the exilic situation in which the tradition of the sacrifices had to be put together and systematized as a program for a new beginning, but also in view of a deficit in the traditions themselves. Should its origins lie in the time of the deuteronomic centralization of the cult, it would be the priestly analogy to those tendencies. At some time the corpus must have become controlled by the Aaronide priestly denomination and its claims. One of the needs for it, in view of a deficit in the traditional sacrificial system, may have been the standardization of legitimate sacrifices and sacrificial procedures *vis-à-vis* a variety of traditional procedures, e.g., the difference between a sacrificing lay person alone and the prerogatives of a priest in the same ritual. Another need may have been the institutional centralization of the sacrificial system and its procedures, which would be mirrored in the systemized integration of the literary corpus. Last but not least, the composition in literary form is in itself an expression of definitiveness. It becomes authoritative, and a control-mechanism for the future of the sacrificial system.

Within and scarcely without such a scenario, the purpose of the prescribed procedures for the individual sacrifices, including Lev 1:3−9, should be considered. The usage of the case law form in each sacrificial type depends on its generic usage in all types of the corpus. It is corpus-systemic. Its purpose is, as in all case laws, to define prescriptively the case of the sacrificial type and its procedure. Within it, the protasis points not so much, at least not primarily, to instruction or information about the availability of a certain sacrifice − everyone knows that − but to the identification of a sacrificial type for which procedure is subse-

---

[78] While Koch's judgment of *Zerschreibung* can be now be left aside because it refers to the literary dissolution of originally oral series, his statement about the composition of the Sinai legislation under *systematic* (his emphasis) aspects, especially in the transmission from the oral to the written stage (1959: 99) is not only exactly to the point; it also applies specifically to the systematization of the sacrificial laws.

quently prescribed in case somebody desires or needs to offer that sacrifice. The protasis does not teach a case; it identifies it, however it is taught, and whether or not it is taught or communicated. The apodosis standardizes the essential steps for the performance of the procedure at the central sanctuary. It is procedure oriented, and serves that standardization to which the offerer is subject together with the priest, so that the purpose of his actual sacrifice may be accomplished.

The question of instruction is thereby no dead issue. The text's purpose of standardizing and systematizing the prescriptions for procedure does not mean that it may not be taught. This may happen through its reading before assemblies of worshippers in settings quite apart from those involving an individual's pilgrimage for personal reasons. It may happen (although it is less likely) through its reading to an individual offerer before his performance. Or it may be studied by priestly students in preparation for their own sacrificial service but with specific attention to the guidance of lay persons through an offering procedure. The primary purpose of the prescription of procedure means only that it aims at securing the standardized and, in that sense, legitimate performance itself, to whatever extent and at whatever place and time it is taught.

It has been said that these prescriptions are *Handlungsanweisungen*. It is probably not coincidental that the term *Handlungsanweisung* was either the cause for or the result of the understanding of the intention of our texts as *Belehrung,* "instruction." To be sure, these texts speak about *Handlungen,* "actions." Yet the term *Anweisung,* "instruction," is ambiguous. *Anweisung zur Handlung* may mean instruction for action or performance, but it may also mean prescription, *"Vorschrift,"* of performance. While the two meanings are not unrelated and can coincide, they are not necessarily identical. When each meaning is considered in its distinctiveness, "prescription," *"Vorschrift,"* focuses on the prescribed *subject-matter,* in our case: on *what* must be done, on the prescribed *content* which includes the actants who have to do it. Such a prescription may be, and in our case is, a law, whereby a law is at any rate prescriptive. By comparison, "instruction," *"Anweisung,"* focuses on the actants themselves, telling them about what is prescribed, or instructing them about a law. In our texts, the subject-matter of legal prescription is certainly ritual performance. But the aspect of envisioned cases of actual ritual performance does not mean that these prescriptive texts are instructing texts. In sum, the texts to which our specific text belongs are prescriptions for future cases of sacrifices rather than instructions to persons for such procedures. And the remaining, and open, question is not primarily if and how these prescriptions were taught, but whether and if so, how, they were in fact observed in the subsequent history of Israel's sacrificial cult. This question, however, transcends the scope of the exegetical study of texts, because it calls for evidence for the actual cultic practice rather than for what the texts prescribed for it.

Postscript. On K. Koch's "Alttestamentliche und altorientalische Rituale"

After completion of the present typescript, Koch's essay appeared in the *Festschrift* for R. Rendtorff. Rather than commenting on this essay throughout my already completed manuscript, I prefer − except for the discussion of Lev 1:9a in the excursus in § 13, section 5 − to combine in this postscript those points that focus on the different results in our studies concerning a genre Ritual in the sense postulated by R. Rendtorff and K. Koch even as their own specifications differ.

K. Koch supports R. Rendtorff's defense of this genre in his just started Leviticus commentary. His major supportive arguments rest on the assumptions of 1) "Schritt für Schritt *rite*" performance; 2) the compositional unity of the final form of the texts which is governed by the order of the sequence of the ritual acts *(Folgehandlungen);* especially 3) the *de facto* existing exceptional *waw* perf. style which is also found in Exod 12; 25ff., and Deut 12 and 26; and 4) the traditio-historical precedence of the claimed genre in Babylonia.

It cannot be denied that germane to a cult-religion − and not to such an institution alone − are "Begehungen, die Schritt für Schritt *rite* durchgeführt werden, nur durch bevollmächtigte Personen und ohne Abweichungen nach spontanen Regungen" (Koch, 1990: 75), and that in regulations for such cultic procedures − and not alone in those − it "wird minutiös geregelt, was an Einzelaktionen unerläßlich ist und durch wen es geschehen muß" (75). Koch's expressions "Schritt für Schritt" and "minutiös" are similar to Rendtorff's *"genau* beschrieben." They are supposed to explain the texts' interest in *"rite."*

Obviously, however, the fact that institutions practice and prescribe acts to be performed *rite* does not *eo ipso* mean that our *texts* are therefore interested in, let alone expressive of, what we call *rite.* Whether or not the texts are governed by or express such an interest, and for that reason may or may not be identified as *Rituale*, depends on the signals for their generic identification found in the texts themselves and not on the fact that institutions practice rites, *"Riten,"* and prescribe, describe, or report about rituals either in a generic form distinct for *Rituale*, a ritual-specific form, or in a different generic form. Although Koch does not address the distinction between performed *Ritus* ("rite") and prescribed *Ritual* (*"prescription* for a rite"), nor the distinction between an assumed specific form for a genre Ritual and alternative generic options for texts pre- or describing ritual procedures, it must be acknowledged that his advocacy of a genre Ritual refers essentially to the signals for it to be found in the texts.

The problem centers, then, above all on our different assessments of the signals in the texts. My own analyses submitted in this publication have resulted in serious reservations concerning the assumption of an exactly or minutely descriptive nature of the prescriptions, and in more than serious doubts about their interest in describing an order of subsequent actions, Koch's "Schritt für Schritt," (1990: 75) understood as "Folgehandlungen" (79). If the aspects of exact or minute ("minutiös") description of the individual acts, and of "Schritt für Schritt" description for the sequential order of the procedures are to be criteria for a genre Ritual prescribing *rite* performance, the texts confirm these criteria far less than is necessary.

The issue of *rite* is also affected by the question of whether the meaning of *rite* performance, performance according to order or custom or prescription, is intrinsic to what must be done, or whether a prescription to perform an act focuses on the act as such, on *what* must be done, while not yet implying, let alone explicitly specifying, that the act must also be performed *rite*, namely, in a specific way. The Latin word *rite* is used in phrases as an attributive or adverbial addition to words, nouns or verbs, about actions. It points to a particular kind of way in which an expressed action must be performed. The two statements "something must be done" and "something must be done *rite*" neither say nor mean the same. While the former statement only refers to the performance of the act, the latter refers formally to its orderly performance without, however, already explicating the kind of performance. The addition of the adverb *"rite"* to the word for the action presupposes the distinction between an act as such and its performance according to a particular order. Our texts only prescribe the acts. They may presuppose *rite* performance implicitly, but they do not say so. Again, if the notion of *rite* is, among other things, supposed to be constitutive for a genre Ritual, the identification of such a genre would in this respect only rest on our assumptions of the text's inexplicit presuppositions — but not at least also on the signals of the texts themselves — a questionable basis for a genre definiton.

Indeed, Koch provides an example for the distinction in a text between the act as such and its specification as *rite*. He quotes a text from the so-called "babylonisch-syrischen Ritualen" (1990: 82) in which the second line says: "Ein Kochöfchen stellst du *rite* auf *(tukani)*." By expressing both what must be done and that it must be done *rite,* this line explicitly distinguishes between the act and its *rite* performance, whereby the latter refers to a particular activity in the performance of the prescribed act. This reference to a specification is apparently necessary — unless one assumes a pleonastic formulation. And it is made in this line only. However, the formal specification *"rite"* is not explicated because the addressee is — again apparently — presupposed to know how to perform this act. Thus, while lines 2–4 of this text prescribe ritual acts, the prescribed acts do not appear to be meant as intrinsically *rite*. And while these lines prescribe the ritual procedure in a case introduced in line 1, the identification of their genre — apart from the role of line 1 for the question of the genre of the entire text — does not rest on the notion of *rite*. For a generic text based on this notion, one would at least for the second line have to assume a separate, in this case possibly presupposed, text, if any at all, which stipulates the specific mode of what in our extant text is referred to as *rite*. Such a text would have to be different in content and composition as well.

Nor does Koch's four-liner show in its entirety that it belongs to a genre Ritual. Its first line, "Wenn *(enuma)* du die Rituale des Šurpu durchführst," uses itself the term "ritual" *(kikittû)*. The use of this word may refer to *prescription* for a ritual performance, ritual in the sense: "Wenn du die [*Vorschriften* für die] Riten, 'rites,' durchführst." Or it may refer to actual ritual performance in the sense: "Wenn du die Riten, 'rites,' durchführst." In either case, the word *"Rituale"* in this text refers to something other than the line in which it is used. If it refers to *prescriptions* for *Riten,* "rites," it must presuppose the existence of (a) generic text(s), oral or written, which do(es) not include the introductory line of our extant text. At best, but not necessarily, such a presupposed text may be introduced by a statement such as: "This is/These are the prescription(s) for the rite of. . . ." It may even be quoted in lines 2–4 of Koch's example. But it would in its entirety not be introduced by the "Wenn"-clause in line 1 of that example, and not structured as a protasis followed by its apodosis. If the word "ritual" in line 1 refers to actual ritual performance itself, to *Ritus,* it refers to a generic setting, and the question of whether that performance is described or prescribed in the genre Ritual or in a different genre is open. To whichever of these two options the word "ritual" in line 1 refers, it refers in neither case to the generic structure and identity of the text in which it stands. In fact, its occurence in this text indicates, among other things, the text's distance and difference from the form of a genre Ritual. The fact that this text uses the word "ritual" does not mean that it belongs to a genre Ritual.

Similarly, Koch quotes one of twenty "Beschwörungsritualen an Ištar und Dumuzi" (1990: 83). This literary unit consists of an expanded protasis introducing a case, and an apodosis in which the prescriptions proper for the case are superscribed by: "Ritual dafür" *(kikiṭṭašu).* In this text, too, the superscription "Ritual dafür" may refer either to the following prescription itself or, more probably, to the ritual perform-ance of the following prescription. In either case, it identifies as Ritual what is either said or referred to in the following apodosis proper, but not in the entire extant text in which it is used. This text, too, clearly signals its generic distance from text-structures for which a genre Ritual is claimed.

Of course, Koch recognizes that "Zur Reihung solcher Anweisungen tritt häufig eine Wenn-Einleitung mit Umstandsangaben und eine Ergebnisfeststellung als Abschluss" (1990: 83). He also asserts that there are *"Du"* as well as *"Er" Rituale* (84) to which the texts in Exod 25 ff. also belong. On the latter issue, it should be admitted that the alternation between second and third pers. forms may belong to a claimed genre Ritual because it can be found within the ritual prescriptions proper and points to functional rather than generic differences within such prescrip-tions. This alternation indicates, therefore, that the second and third pers. forms are relative, i.e., not constitutive for the identity of the claimed genre, which of course also means that they do not speak against it. More important is the fact that neither the *Du* nor the *Er* form are self-evident signals for such a genre. They are used in different genres as well, and it depends on criteria other than these grammatical forms whether they belong to one genre or another, or whether in a conflation of genres, e.g., of law and instruction, one dominates the other. As for the instructions for the construction of the sanctuary in Exod 25 ff., the second pers. form may, therefore, belong to a genre Ritual if those texts belong to such a genre. However, sufficient evidence for that claim has not been established. The claim above all would have to demonstrate, in critical comparison with the objectives of other ritual prescriptions, why descriptions or prescriptions of the construction of a building, as well as the reports about the execution of such construction, even of a sanctuary, themselves generic, are to be identified as *Rituale*.

More problematic for the claim of a genre Ritual is the inclusion of the protasis clauses into the text basis. This inclusion amounts to more than another example of the variability of structural elements within a typical text basis discerned for the identification of a genre. It amounts to a new typical text basis and, hence, points to a different genre, originally oral or written. Koch himself affirms the importance of the text basis when confirming Rendtorff's focus on "der kompositorischen Einheit der Endgestalt des Textes" (1990: 77). For Rendtorff's studies, including his most recent Leviticus commentary, and for Koch's original study on Exod 26–Lev 16, the text basis for the claimed genre Ritual excludes the protases for known and definitive reasons. The typical textual unity for the claimed genre consists of the prescriptions directly and originally alone. For the exegesis of the texts about rituals in Leviticus, this has meant that their protases had to be explained either literary critically as secondary or as case law imitations by way of a protasis, or as *Verschriftung* – so Koch against Rendtorff.

However, the separation of the protases from their apodoses has proved difficult to substantiate, and it becomes virtually impossible as we insist on assessing a genre on the basis of the compositional unity of extant texts and, I should add, on the generic typicalities of this unity. As for the first unit in Lev 1, the consideration of genre can, therefore, no longer isolate vv. 4–9 based on the perf. forms. It will have to rest on vv. 2aβ + b and 3aα + 3aβ–9. This has not been assumed by Rendtorff in his Leviticus commentary for the defense of a genre Ritual. If the protases are included, the basis for his defended genre has disappeared, and the question of genre is in principle open because of a new, typical structural basis of the texts for which both the protases and apodoses, and their intrinsic correlation, represent two distinctly different yet equally important components which constitute the macro-structures of these text units. These texts belong to an *allo genos,* namely, the genre of case law. Koch's quotations of the Babylonian texts (1990: 82, 83) confirm this result. In these texts, too, the protases are the first equally important component of a bipartite generic structure, rather than an occasional introduction variably added to an otherwise constituted generic structure. Moreover, these texts demonstrate the distinction between their own generic case law form and, explicitly, their reference to the rituals prescribed in parts of them, regardless whether their word "ritual" refers to ritual performance, *Ritus,* or to a prescriptive genre Ritual for which a text basis would have to be assumed that differs from the basis of the texts at hand. The texts at hand are case laws *about* rituals.

Finally, if the protases are included for the identification of genre, the presence of the perf. forms in the apodoses can scarcely remain a predominant, let alone the sole, argument in favor of a genre Ritual. The perf. form has been, and still is in Rendtorff's *Leviticus,* the decisive argument in defense of that genre, inevitably at the expense of the broader final text base that includes the protases. He retains that argument – after abandoning literary critical criteria – by explaining the imperf. form, e.g., in 1:9aα, as a signal for *Nebenhandlungen* (although his determination of *Nebenhandlungen* is not confined to sentences in the imperf. form!). Koch's insistence in the facticity of the perf. forms and their exceptionality is in order (1990: 79). But his contention that this stylistic factor should be the sole explanation for "das Postulat einer besonderen Gattung" (79) still provokes more questions than it solves. This factor may as well be characteristic of the style of a particular group, or of priestly and deuteronomic groups, who employed that style in different genres for reasons other than signaling a specific genre.

It seems that one of the distinctions that must be further clarified in exegetical work is the distinction within texts, especially extant texts, between their explicit reference to or their substantive focus on rituals and their own varying generic nature. Texts *about* rituals are not for that reason *Rituale.* That may be the case. Whether or not it is so depends not only on the fact that they must speak about rituals, but on the dominant signals by which genres can be identified. In our interpretations of the ritual texts in Leviticus, we thus far differ on which signals are dominant, or constitutive, for the identification of their genre. Work on the problem will certainly have to continue, and I am confident that in that, too, we will be together.[79]

---

[79] The two Babylonian texts quoted by K. Koch and referred to in this discussion were published by E. Reiner und W. Farber. For the data of their publication, see the bibliography of this study.

Bibliography

BARTELMUS, R. (1989), "pātaḥ." Cols. 831–852 in *TWAT* Vol. 6

BLUM, E. (1984), *Die Komposition der Vätergeschichte*. WMANT 57. Neukirchen-Vluyn: Neukirchener Verlag

BRICHTO, H. C. (1976), "On Slaughter and Sacrifice, Blood and Atonement." *HUCA* 47: 19–55

ELLIGER, K. (1966), *Leviticus*. HAT 4. Tübingen: J. C. B. Mohr

FARBER, W. (1977), "AAWLM." Pp. 236–46 in *Beschwörungsrituale an Ištar und Dumuzi*. Veröffentlichungen d. Orient. Kommission 30. Wiesbaden: Steiner

GERLEMAN, G. (1976), "rṣh." Cols. 810–813 in *THAT* Vol. 2

GRUBER, M. L. (1987), "Women in the Cult According to the Priestly Code." Pp. 35–48 in *Judaic Perspectives on Ancient Israel*. Ed. J. Neusner, B. Levine, and E. Frerichs. Philadelphia: Fortress

HUTTON, R. R. (1983), "Declaratory Formulae: Forms of Authoritative Pronouncement in Ancient Israel." Diss., Claremont Graduate School

JANOWSKI, B. (1982), *Sühne als Heilsgeschehen*. WMANT 55. Neukirchen-Vluyn: Neukirchener Verlag

KIUCHI, N. (1987), *The Purification Offering in the Priestly Literature: Its Meaning and Function*. JSOTSup 56. Sheffield: University of Sheffield

KNIERIM, R. P. (1985), "The Composition of the Pentateuch." Pp. 393–415 in *Society of Biblical Literature Seminar Papers* 24

– (1990), "The Book of Numbers." Pp. 155–163 in *Die Hebräische Bibel und ihre zweifache Nachgeschichte. Festschrift für Rolf Rendtorff zum 65. Geburtstag*. Ed. E. Blum, C. Macholz, and E. Stegemann. Neukirchen-Vluyn: Neukirchener Verlag

KOCH, K. (1959), *Die Priesterschrift von Exodus 25 bis Leviticus 16*. FRLANT 71. Göttingen: Vandenhoeck & Ruprecht

– (1966), and Bo Reicke. "Stiftshütte." Cols. 1871–1875 in *Biblisch-Historisches Handwörterbuch*. 4 vols. Ed. B. Reicke and L. Rost. Göttingen: Vandenhoeck & Ruprecht

– (1986), "nîḥôaḥ." Cols. 442–445 in *TWAT* Vol. 5

– (1990), "Alttestamentliche und altorientalische Rituale." Pp. 75–85 in *Die Hebräische Bibel und ihre zweifache Nachgeschichte. Festschrift für Rolf Rendtorff zum 65. Geburtstag*. Neukirchen-Vluyn: Neukirchener Verlag

LEVINE, B. A. (1989), *Leviticus*. JPS Torah Commentary. Philadelphia: Jewish Publication Society

LIEDKE, G. (1971), *Gestalt und Bezeichnung alttestamentlicher Rechtssätze*. WMANT 39. Neukirchen-Vluyn: Neukirchener Verlag

MILGROM, J. (1970), *Studies in Levitical Terminology, I: the Encroacher and the Levite, the term 'Aboda*. University of California Publications, Near Eastern Studies 14. Berkley: University of California

– (1976), "Sacrifices and Offerings, OT." Pp. 763–771 in *The Interpreter's Dictionary of the Bible: Supplementary Volume*. Nashville: Abingdon

– (1983), *Studies in Cultic Theology and Terminology*. Studies in Judaism in Late Antiquity 36. Leiden: E. J. Brill

– (1990), *Numbers*. JPS Torah Commentary. Philadelphia: Jewish Publication Society

NOTH, M. (1959), *Das zweite Buch Mose: Exodus*. ATD 5. Göttingen: Vandenhoeck & Ruprecht

– (1962), *Das dritte Buch Mose: Leviticus*. ATD 6. Göttingen: Vandenhoeck & Ruprecht

PEDERSEN, J. (1926–40), *Israel: Its Life and Culture*. 4 vols. London: Oxford University

VON RAD, G. (1958), "Die Anrechnung des Glaubens zur Gerechtigkeit." Pp. 130–135 in *Gesammelte Studien zum Alten Testament*. Vol. 1. Theologische Bücherei 8. Munich: Chr. Kaiser

REINER, E. (1958), *Šurpu: A Collection of Sumerian and Akkadian Incantations*. Archiv für Orientforschung 11. Graz.

RENDTORFF, R. (1954), *Die Gesetze in der Priesterschrift*. FRLANT 62. Göttingen: Vandenhoeck & Ruprecht

– (1967), *Studien zur Geschichte des Opfers im Alten Israel*. WMANT 24. Neukirchen-Vluyn: Neukirchener Verlag

– (1985), *Leviticus*. Biblischer Kommentar: Altes Testament 3/1. Neukirchen-Vluyn: Neukirchener Verlag

RIGBY, P. (1980), "A Structural Analysis of Israelite Sacrifice and Its Other Institutions." *Église et théologie* 11: 299–351

RODRIGUEZ, A. M. (1979), *Substitution in the Hebrew Cultus*. Berrien Springs: Andrews University Press

SCHOTTROFF, W. (1971), "*ḥšb.*" Cols. 641–646 in *THAT* Vol. 1

SEYBOLD, K. (1982), "*ḥāšab.*" Cols. 243–261 in *TWAT* Vol. 3

STOLZ, F. (1976a), "*nūᵃḥ.*" Cols. 43–46 in *THAT* Vol. 2

– (1976b), "*smk.*" Cols. 160–162 in *THAT* Vol. 2

TURNER, V. W. (1969), *The Ritual Process*. New York: Aldine

UTZSCHNEIDER, H. (1988), *Das Heiligtum und das Gesetz*. OBO 77. Göttingen: Vandenhoeck & Ruprecht

WENHAM, G. J. (1979), *The Book of Leviticus*. NICOT 3. Grand Rapids: Wm. B. Eerdmans

WRIGHT, A., J. MILGROM, and H.-J. FABRY (1986), "*sāmak.*" Cols. 880–889 in *TWAT* Vol. 5

Scripture Index

Subject Index

Hebrew Word Index

Author Index

Reinhard Gregor Kratz

Kyros im Deuterojesaja-Buch

Redaktionsgeschichtliche Untersuchungen zu Entstehung und Theologie von Jes 40—55

Die Kyros-Aussagen im Jesajabuch spielen eine entscheidende Rolle bei der Erklärung von Jes 40—55 als einem separaten Textbereich, für den sich die Bezeichnung Deuterojesaja eingebürgert hat. Sie werden fast einhellig zu den zentralen Verkündigungsinhalten von Buch und dahinter vermutetem Propheten gerechnet. An ihnen bricht denn auch die deuterojesajanische Frage in aller Schärfe auf, die die Forschung seit Entdeckung des Buches begleitet hat und heute besonders kontrovers diskutiert wird: Wie erklärt sich die Einheitlichkeit der Schrift, die sich doch aus vielen einzelnen Worteinheiten zusammensetzt? Die hier vorgelegte Analyse der Kyros-Texte und der literarischen Kontexte im Dtjes-Buch macht deutlich, daß es sich dabei weder um eine nur zufällige Sammlung von Einzelworten noch um eine einheitliche, planvoll durchgestaltete Komposition handeln kann, wie vielfach behauptet wird. Vielmehr wird schon in den Kyros-Texten eine literarische Schichtung wahrgenommen, die sich auf verschiedenen Ebenen durch das ganze Buch hindurch verfolgen läßt.

Die Spannung von Einheitlichkeit und Komplexität im Dtjes-Buch findet so in dem Modell der kontextgebundenen Fortschreibungs- und Auslegungsgeschichte eine neuartige Erklärung. Außer der Analyse der Kyros-Texte möchte die Arbeit auf diesem Wege Einsichten in das Werden des ganzen Buches, speziell noch in die Götzen-, die Ebed-Texte und ihre buchinterne Auslegung sowie in den Vorgang der Fortschreibung an sich vermitteln, in dem sich die Entwicklung und Entfaltung der ›deuterojesajanischen‹ Theologie(n) vollzogen hat.

1991. X, 254 Seiten (Forschungen zum Alten Testament 1). Leinen.

J. C. B. (Paul Siebeck) Tübingen